Pakistan Occupied
Kashmir

The Untold Story

Attention Authors

Manas Publications is fighting a war to tell the world that India can win the battle not only by bullet but also by pen. We are converting fighters into writers since there is no dearth of intellectuals in our country but their knowledge is confined to them only. No sincere effort has been made by any other publisher to give the right direction to their knowledge and the talent of an intellectual is lying hidden. An author always gives the raw material in the shape of manuscript and it is the sense of a publisher to make it a finished product. We are motivating the intellectuals' mind and publishing their manuscripts for more than two decades and would like to publish your manuscript too. If you or your colleagues have any manuscript or are working on it, please don't hesitate to contact us with detailed synopsis and contents for its publication. We take utmost care in production and give a wide publicity to the book and its author. We can also suggest you the title for the writing related to your subject, as we are the publishers who believe more in quality than in quantity.

Pakistan Occupied
Kashmir

The Untold Story

Editors

Virendra Gupta

Deputy Director
Institute for Defence Studies and Analyses (IDSA)

and

Alok Bansal

Research Fellow: IDSA

INSTITUTE FOR DEFENCE STUDIES AND ANALYSES
NEW DELHI

Manas Publications

New Delhi-110002 (INDIA)

Manas Publications

(Publishers, Distributors, Importers & Exporters)
4858, Prahlad Street,
24, Ansari Road, Darya Ganj,
New Delhi - 110 002 (INDIA)
Ph.: 23260783, 23265523:, 23842660 (R)
Fax: 011-23272766
E-mail: manaspublications@vsnl.com

© Institute for Defence Studies and Analysis (IDSA)
2007

ISBN 81-7049-315-3
Rs. 495/-

Typeset at
Manas Publications

Printed in India at
Nice Printing Press, Delhi
and Published by Mrs. Suman Lata for
Manas Publications,
4858, Prahlad Street,
24, Ansari Road, Darya Ganj,
New Delhi - 110 002 (INDIA).

Preface

It has been nearly six decades since tribal raiders aided and abetted by Pakistani Army stormed into the princely state of Jammu and Kashmir (J&K). The aim of the operation was to either depose Maharaja Hari Singh— the then ruler of the sovereign state of Jammu and Kashmir— and annex the state, or force him to accede to Pakistan. Under the force of circumstances, however, the Maharaja instead decided to accede to India and requested for military help to evict the raiders. It is worth noting that there was overwhelming popular support for the king's decision. While the raiders were successfully pushed out of Kashmir Valley, a significant portion of the former state of Jammu and Kashmir however, continues to remain under Pakistani occupation. In terms of territory, the area under Pakistan's occupation is 78,114 sq. kilometres out of the total area of 222,236 sq. kilometres comprising the state of Jammu and Kashmir. Despite the expansion of electronic media and 24 X 7 news coverage, there is a surprising lack of knowledge about this region, which is under Pakistan's illegal occupation, not only in India but also the world at large.

People often tend to use the term 'Azad Kashmir' for Pakistan Occupied Kashmir (POK), but it needs to be understood that the two are not the same. POK is the total area under Pakistani occupation, which has been further divided by Pakistan into the so called "Azad Jammu and Kashmir (AJK)" comprising Mirpur district of Jammu, bulk of the old *Jagir* of Poonch, and a portion of the North Western Kashmir province, which constitutes less than 15 per cent of the territory under Pakistani occupation; and the sparsely populated 'Northern Areas', an amorphous entity governed directly by Islamabad, which constitutes more than 85 per cent of POK. Under the Boundary Agreement between Pakistan and China concluded in March 1963, Pakistan unilaterally ceded to China, more than 5180 sq. kilometres of the territory belonging to the former state of Hunza, under its illegal occupation, ignoring objections from both the *Mir* of Hunza and India.

While the Indo-Pak conflict over Jammu and Kashmir remains in limelight, the social and political developments in 'AJK' and its relations with Pakistan receive scant attention. In notional terms, 'AJK' has the status of an 'autonomous' state. It has an 'interim' constitution, which provides for a parliamentary form of government with a president as the constitutional head; a prime minister as the chief executive; and a forty-eight-member legislative assembly; a judiciary with Supreme and High Courts; an election commission; and even its own national anthem and flag. Nevertheless, for all practical purposes, 'AJK' is governed by Islamabad through its Ministry of Kashmir Affairs and Northern Areas (KANA) and the 'Azad Jammu and Kashmir' Council (since 1974). Given the immense strategic significance of Gilgit-Baltistan(Northern Areas), Pakistan has kept it separate from 'Azad Kashmir' and controls it directly.

While Kashmir is being projected as an inter-state dispute and a nuclear flashpoint by some, the genesis of the conflict is conveniently forgotten. Moreover, in the discourses on Kashmir, the other part of Kashmir, which is under Pakistani control, is seldom mentioned. The political developments within POK are rarely monitored. It is also not very well known that the people of POK are critical of the step-motherly approach of the central Pakistani administration towards them and that they have started demanding genuine self-administration in both 'Azad Jammu

Preface

and Kashmir' and 'Northern Areas'. There is a need to increase awareness about the political processes, events and developments in the POK, so as to facilitate an objective assessment of the problems confronting the people in the region. In this context, it is significant that Baroness Emma Nicholson in her report to the European Parliament has highlighted the lack of democratic rights enjoyed by the residents in POK. Similarly, the Human Rights Watch has also lamented the lack of basic human rights in POK.

The present book is a compilation of eleven analytical papers by contributors known for their interest and expertise on Kashmir. These papers analyse developments in October 1947 leading to Kashmir's accession to India, the pattern of administration that evolved in 'AJK' and the 'Northern Areas' over the years and current developments in these territories. The papers are analytical and base their arguments on facts. The rise of ethnicity and fundamentalism in Pakistan has had its impact in POK. The growing fundamentalism has led to Talibanisation of the society and has accentuated the sectarian divide. This book is an attempt to highlight the State of Affairs in POK.

In his paper, Parvez Dewan analyses political developments in 'AJK' since December 1946 and comes to the conclusion that Pakistan has ensured its absolute control over the government in 'AJK' by perpetuating an over-centralised power-relation between Muzaffarabad and Islamabad. The paper by Smruti Pattanaik also examines these unequal power relations and concludes that the interim constitution of 1974 has reduced 'AJK' to an insignificant appendage of the Pakistani state. The account by Maloy Krishna Dhar acquaints us with the present day political climate in 'Azad Kashmir' and the 'Northern Areas'. Dhar argues that Pakistan has used this territory effectively against Indian interests. He draws attention to the military build-up by Pakistan through construction of elaborate roads, airstrips and high altitude training centres in POK after the

Kargil war. The articles by P. Stobdan, Alok Bansal, Samuel Baid and Shafqat Inqalabi make exhaustive analyses of the pre-independence history of Gilgit-Baltistan, the way it was annexed by Pakistan and the condition of the people under direct rule by Pakistan.

The Indian approach to the Kashmir issue has been well covered by S Kalyanaraman and Virendra Gupta in their papers. Kalyanaraman focuses on the tribal raid and argues that while Pakistan planned the raid and executed it through serving officers in Pakistani army, India insisted on the Maharaja to introduce responsible and representative administration in Kashmir.

In his article on Indus Water Treaty, B. G. Vergese makes a forceful argument in favour of an Indus II agreement, based on the existing Indus treaty, which along with other measures like soft border, bilateral trade and cultural exchanges can lay the basis for effective peace making between India and Pakistan. This will go a long way in defusing the Kashmir dispute through increased people to people interaction and increased trade and commerce across the line of control.

We would like to acknowledge our gratitude to all our distinguished contributors and Shri NS Sisodia, Director IDSA, who encouraged us to come out with this publication. We would also like to thank our colleagues, Dr Ashok Behuria and Dr Sreeradha Datta, for their valuable assistance in the editing of this book.

Virendra Gupta
Alok Bansal

Contents

The Contributors

Virendra Gupta: Virendra Gupta is a serving career diplomat from the Indian Foreign Service and has served abroad in Indian Missions in Nepal, Nigeria, Israel and Egypt, in various capacities. He has also served in the Indian Mission to the United Nations, where he served as Rapporteur of the United Nations Special Committee against Apartheid. He has also been Deputy Secretary (UN) and Director (Disarmament) at the Ministry of External Affairs in New Delhi. He has been India's High Commissioner to Tanzania and Trinidad and Tobago. He is currently the Deputy Director of IDSA on deputation from MEA and writes regularly for newspapers on issues concerning South Asia.

P Stobdan: Phunchok Stobdan is a leading Indian expert on issues concerning national and international security with specific focus on Asian affairs covering Central Asia and Inner Asia, including Xinjiang, Tibet, Myanmar and the Himalayan region. He holds an M Phil degree from School of International Studies, Jawaharlal Nehru University, New Delhi and has written extensively on a wide range of security-related subjects in a number of professional journals on strategic affairs, books and newspapers both in India and abroad. He served in Central Asia as the Director of the Indian Cultural Centre at the Embassy of India, Almaty, Kazakhstan between 1999 and 2002. He has also served as Joint Director in the Indian National Security Council. He is a Senior Fellow at IDSA currently on lien to Jammu University, where he is the Director/ Professor, Centre for Strategic and Regional Studies.

S. Kalyanaraman: S. Kalyanaraman holds a PhD in International Relations from Jawaharlal Nehru University, New Delhi. He was awarded the Nehru Centenary British Fellowship and has served as a Visiting Fellow at the Department of War Studies, Kings College, London. He has worked at the United Service Institution of India, New Delhi. He is presently a Research Fellow at the Institute for Defence Studies and Analyses (IDSA), New Delhi. He is the Editor of the *IDSA Strategic Comments,* published on the IDSA website and a member of the Editorial Board of the IDSA· journal *Strategic Analysis.* He is currently involved in studying the wars India has fought since independence. His publications include: "The Indian Way in Counter-insurgency" in Efraim Inbar, ed., *Democracies and Small Wars* (Frank Cass: London, 2003); "Operation Parakram: An Indian Exercise in Coercive Diplomacy," *Strategic Analysis,* October-December 2002.

Alok Bansal: Commander Alok Bansal is a serving officer with 24 years of commissioned service in Indian Navy. He has served in a number of Naval and Coast Guard ships and has commanded two naval ships. He has participated in Op Pawan in Srilanka. He has been a Directing Staff at the Defence Services Staff College Wellington for three years. He holds an M Sc and M Phil degree in Defence and Strategic Studies from the University of Madras and is currently pursuing doctorate from School of International Studies, Jawaharlal Nehru University, New Delhi. He is currently a Research Fellow with the IDSA and is a part of Southern Asia Cluster. He is working on Internal disorders in Pakistan. His other areas of interest include Indian Ocean Region, Indian Diaspora and Maritime Issues.

Parvez Dewan: Parvez Dewan is the Chairman of the India Tourism Development Corporation (ITDC). An IAS officer of the Jammu and Kashmir cadre, he studied at St Stephen's College, Delhi, where he won the L. Raghubir Singh History Prize for ranking 1st in the class. At the University of Cambridge he was awarded the Jennings Prize for obtaining the highest marks and a congratulatory distinction in Development Studies. He has authored two books about the Names of Allah, a trilogy about Hanuman ji and an encyclopaedic trilogy about Jammu, Kashmir and Ladakh. Parvez Dewan has been elected Visiting Research Fellow of Queen Elizabeth House, Oxford University.

Maloy Krishna Dhar: Maloy Krishna Dhar, served the Intelligence Bureau, India's prime intelligence agency for nearly three decades, during which he conducted and witnessed innumerable counter-terrorism, counter-espionage and political operations. He specialized in counter-intelligence measures to meet Pakistan's overt and covert aggression and proxy war it had unleashed against India. He retired as its Joint Director. After retirement he has taken up freelance journalism and professional writing. He has written a number of books, which include two books of fiction "Mission to Pakistan—An Intelligence agent in Pakistan" and "Bitter Harvest". He also co-authored "Pakistan After 9/11". His recent publications are "Open Secrets: India's Intelligence Unveiled" and "Fulcrum of Evil: ISI-CIA-Al Qaeda Nexus".

Samuel Baid: Samuel Baid holds a degree in English from Delhi University and a degree in journalism from Punjab University. He established the Pakistan Desk in UNI in November 1971 in the run up to the liberation of Bangladesh and headed it for a number of years. His desk put out on UNI, wire stories that frequently made headlines in national dailies. He started the world's first Urdu news service on Teleprinter for UNI in 1992 and was the editor of UNI's Urdu service till his retirement in 1998. He has written numerous papers and articles on Pakistan for journals and newspapers. He has also co-authored a book "Pakistan: An End Without Beginning". He is currently director of YMCA's Institute for Media Studies and Information Technology at New Delhi.

Smruti S Pattanaik: Smruti S Pattanaik holds a PhD in International Relations from South Asian Studies Division of

Jawaharlal Nehru University. She was awarded the Kodikara Fellowship by the Regional Centre for Strategic Studies, Colombo in 1999. The study has been published as "Elite Perceptions in Foreign Policy: Role of Print Media in Influencing Indo-Pak Relations, 1989-99". She also received Asia Fellowship 2003-2004, administered by the Asian Scholarship Foundation, Bangkok and funded by the Ford Foundation for research on "State Formation in South Asia: Role of Identity and Nationalism in the Making of Bangladesh." She has been granted a follow-up award by the Asian Scholarship Foundation to work on Religion Politics and Islamic militancy in Bangladesh. She is presently a Research Fellow at the Institute for Defence Studies and Analyses, New Delhi and has written extensively on Military and Politics, Issues of Nationalism and National Identity in South Asia.

Shafqat Inqalabi: Shafqat Ali Inqalabi is the spokesperson of Balwaristan National Front. A resident of Bubur in Puniyal Tehsil of Ghizar District in Gilgit-Baltistan, he is a qualified Civil Engineer and had established a district level political party named 'Ghizar National Movement' in 1997. After the party's merger in 'Karakoram National Movement' in 2000, he headed the Karakoram Students Organisation from 2000 to 2003 as its President and from 2003 to 2005 as its Central Chairman. After joining Balwaristan National Front in 2005, he has been its spokesman. He writes columns for local newspapers and magazines and has a regular column in the magazine 'Bang-e-Sehar'. He has written a book of poetry, which is under publication.

BG Verghese: BG Verghese is a veteran journalist, having joined the *Times of India* in 1949. A recipient of Magsaysay Award for Journalism in 1975, he has been the editor of *Hindustan Times* and *Indian Express*. He has been the Information Adviser to the Prime Minister, Information Consultant to the Defence Minister and Member of the National Security Advisory Board and the Kargil Review Committee. He is a Visiting Professor at the Centre for Policy

Research, New Delhi and the Chairman of the Commonwealth Human Rights Initiative and currently holds the Non-Traditional Security Chair under the Delhi Policy Group where he is working on Managing Diversity in the context of insurgency and Maoist Extremism in India. An author of several books, his recent works include a biography of RN Goenka—"Warrior of the Fourth Estate", "Tomorrow's India: Another Tryst with Destiny" and "A J&K Primer: From Myth to Reality".

1

Indo-Pak Relations and the Kashmir Issue

Virendra Gupta

The symbolic handshake by PM Manmohan Singh and Gen Musharraf in Havana in September 2006 did manage to prevent the Indo-Pak peace process from getting derailed. That this happened despite a high pitched rhetoric in India concerning relations with Pakistan is a tribute to Manmohan Singhs' maturity and statesmanship. However, patience and perseverance would be required in both sides for sustenance of this process and its eventual success.

India and Pakistan have shared a difficult relationship right from the inception—Indian independence and the creation of Pakistan. Historians will seek to find answers for what went wrong; whether it has just been a case of sibling rivalry gone bad or was there a more fundamental reason to explain these problems? The 'two-nation theory' propounded by the Muslim League asserted that Hindus and Muslims are two different nations and, therefore, could not stay together.[1] Clearly, this theory on which partition of India was premised was ill-founded, as the subsequent developments have demonstrated. Even Pakistanis have questioned this theory. Altaf Hussain the MQM (Muttahida Qaumi Movement) leader, has debunked the 'two-nation theory' (of India) noting that the partition (of

India) was the "greatest blunder in the history of mankind". In an interview to the Herald in Oct 2000 he stated that this "objective assessment (was) based on the bitter experience of the masses".[2] It is hard to imagine that an elaborate plan was conjured up to separate people merely on the basis of their religion even though it had been well known that Hindu and Muslim populations in undivided India, as indeed is the case in today's India, were completely intermingled (almost every village and town in India has both Hindus and Muslims living together for centuries before the British came to our country) and not segmented in exclusive hamlets as perhaps was the case in Palestine. Decision to divide India could not have been based entirely on its socio-cultural environment? Were there some other vested interests at play? Was India's partition the last act of colonial exploitation in the subcontinent?

India and Pakistan have been engaged in conventional wars (Including the confrontation in Kargil), on several occasions and most of them were fought over Kashmir.[3] The war in 1971 led to the creation of Bangladesh, thereby negating the very basis of two-nation theory and culminated in the historic 'Shimla Agreement.' The understanding reached between the two countries at Shimla was extremely significant in the sense that it put the relations between the two countries in the contextual framework of "conflict and confrontation that hitherto marred their relations". It bound the two countries to respect "the line of control resulting from the ceasefire of Dec 17, 1971" in Jammu and Kashmir (J&K) and sanctified the good neighbourliness through a commitment to resolving their differences only "by peaceful means through bilateral negotiations".[4]

India has clung on to the spirit of Shimla all these years in trying to improve and consolidate its relations with Pakistan in a comprehensive manner. It has sought to build people-to-people contacts through extensive academic and cultural exchanges in the firm belief that people of both the countries really have no problems among themselves (Indians and

Pakistanis living abroad, in fact, get along quite well given their shared cultural values and preferences) and that any exercise in rapprochement must not only involve them but should also begin with them. India has also sought to upgrade the economic and commercial contacts with Pakistan since these perhaps constitute the most important measure of relations between any two countries in the present times. It is the politics which has kept the people of India and Pakistan separated. India's approach has been to downplay the politics of its relations with Pakistan and to focus on deliverables, tangible actions which would contribute to improving the quality of life of people on both sides. India can certainly not be accused of duplicity or double standards since it has followed the same pragmatic approach in its relations with China. The fact that the annual bilateral trade between India and China is poised to reach a phenomenal figure of US $20 billion amply vindicates that approach.

Pakistan, on the other hand, has been insisting that the Kashmir issue must be accorded priority to the exclusion of almost everything else while addressing the contentious issues in the process of normalization of bilateral relations. That approach is not just impractical but seriously flawed as there can not be a quick-fix solution to a longstanding problem such as Kashmir.[5] By maintaining a hardened position on an issue as intractable as Kashmir, and creating a linkage with other issues, Pakistan is letting go of an opportunity to build trust and confidence and better understanding amongst the people which would ultimately help create the requisite favourable environment for bold political decisions in the future. The liberal intellectuals in Pakistan, in fact, suggest that "Kashmir should be put on the back burner for some years. In that period, trade with India should be encouraged, along with travel and cross-border cultural exchanges. As contacts develop between the two rivals, mutual fears would decline. And then Kashmir could be dealt with".[6]

While India was celebrating the apparent bonhomie created both at the level of leadership and at peoples level during Prime Minister Vajpayee's Lahore visit in 1999, a conspiracy was being hatched, quite unknown to it, in the army barracks of Pakistan for a well-orchestrated military intrusion across the Line of Control (LoC) in Kargil. Whether or not Nawaz Sharif was fully into the loop and whether or not Army Chief Musharraf was acting on his own at that time is quite immaterial even as the Kargil issue is still off-hints. "As long as Musharraf stays in power, open discussion of Kargil will remain taboo". [7] What is pertinent to note is that Pakistan's misadventure in Kargil "led to the disruption of the Lahore process" as pointed out by former Pakistan Foreign Minister Sartaj Aziz in a radio interview in London after the release of General Musharraf's book 'In the Line of Fire'. Notably, he also went on to dispute Gen Musharaff's claim in the book that Kargil helped bring Kashmir back to international spotlight.[8]

While India has tried to assiduously preserve the Shimla spirit (even in the face of Kargil incursions by Pakistan, Indian fighter aircrafts were instructed not to cross the Line of Control in J&K), Pakistan has been waging a low intensity war against India by actively funding, coordinating and supporting terrorist activities in J&K and other parts of the country. In fact, the use of cross border terrorism against India has been finely crafted by Pakistan as its state policy. It has negated and undermined its obligations under Shimla agreement not to disturb the LoC, by regularly promoting infiltration into India of terrorists trained in numerous terrorist training camps dotted all across the Pakistan Occupied Kashmir (POK).

In recent years India has emphasised the need to find solutions to problems through bilateral means, but Pakistan has consistently sought to internationalize the Kashmir issue. As part of that strategy, Pakistan routinely raises Kashmir issue at all available international fora including those not specifically concerned with political and security issues. It has also sought to project the Kashmir issue, which is really an issue of blatant Pakistani aggression and illegal occupation of large chunks of Indian territory by use of force, as an 'Islamic issue' by embarking on a massive disinformation campaign. One must give credit to Pakistani diplomacy in the sense that it may have partially succeeded in its designs, particularly if one were to go by the routine reaffirmations of Organization of Islamic Conference (OIC) and hardline Muslim clerics around the world clubbing Kashmir with Palestine and Chechnya. But, one wonders whether it has ever occurred to Pakistan that injecting religion into an essentially non-religious political issue would only serve to make it even more difficult to resolve. If India were to make any concessions in Kashmir- under pressure from the Islamists or in the name of religion, it would have devastating consequences for its delicate socio-cultural fabric which is rooted in plurality and secularism.[9] Pakistani leadership is perceptive enough to realize it. Perhaps, despite its loud advocacy and rhetoric, it is not really a matter of priority for the Pakistani government to find a solution to the Kashmir issue.

Pakistan argues about the sanctity of the UN resolutions on Kashmir. But, it draws attention selectively to only one part of the key August 13, 1948 Resolution of the UN Security Council. It must be noted that that resolution was sequential in nature: in the first part, it called for ceasefire; in the second part, it obligated Pakistan to withdraw from the entire state of Jammu and Kashmir (J&K) its troops as well as "tribesmen and Pakistani nationals not normally resident therein (in J&K) who (had) entered the state for the purpose of fighting"; and, in the last part it provided for the plebiscite to determine the final status of J&K in accordance with the wishes of the people, but only after the completion of the first and second parts, i.e. after withdrawal of Pakistani forces and non-regular combatants from the state and restoration of normalcy. Despite repeated calls by India through the fifties and the sixties, this resolution remained unimplemented because of non-fulfilment by Pakistan of its obligation under the resolution.[10] Truth is, Pakistan could never muster enough courage to withdraw its forces from the state in the fear of losing control over the territory which it had illegally occupied by use of force. It must be remembered that Kashmir always prided itself on its moderate stream of Islam in total contrast to the radical fundamentalist approach of Jinnah's Muslim League and Pakistani government knew it all along that it stood no chance at all in any exercise by the people of J&K of their free will.

It also bears emphasizing that the requirement of plebiscite in the UN resolution was not something 'imposed' upon India; it was merely a reiteration of the voluntary affirmation made by the Government of India while accepting the instrument of accession from the Maharaja of J&K in October 1947. It was of course made quite clear then, as subsequently in the UN resolution, that this could be done only after Pakistani "raiders (were) beaten back and peace (was) restored in Kashmir." It must be noted that even if the subsequent events, emerging out of Pakistan's non-cooperation, prevented the fulfilment of this assurance, there have never been any doubts in legal terms concerning the unconditional accession of J&K state to India. The concept of self-determination as visualized in the UN Charter applies to colonised people and is only as relevant to the people of J&K as it is to the people of Baloochistan in Pakistan.

J&K's accession to India was decided in terms of the legal framework applicable to princely states as contained in the Partition Settlement and Indian Independence Act, passed by British Parliament. All the Princely States were advised by Lord Mountbatten to join either one of the two new Dominions (of India or Pakistan). Although the Congress Party was of the view that the wishes of the people be taken into account, in case of any doubts the Muslim League was insistent that the choice of the Ruler be considered as final.[11] Jinnah in a statement on June 19, 1947, had stated "Indian (princely) states will be independent sovereign states on the termination of (British) paramountcy...it is open to them to join the Hindustan Constituent Assembly or the Pakistan Constituent Assembly, or to decide to remain independent...we do not wish to interfere with the internal affairs of any state, for that is a matter primarily to be resolved between the rulers and the peoples of the states". In legal terms it clearly implies that full discretion was vested in the ruler of a Princely State to sign the instrument of accession for joining either India or Pakistan.[12] In fact, Jammu and Kashmir's accession to India was not at all challenged by the UN Commission for India and Pakistan and it is noteworthy that the US Representative in the UN Security Council stated on February 4, 1948 that "with the accession of J&K to India, this foreign sovereignty (of J&K state) went over to India and is exercised by India and that is how India happens to be here as a petitioner".[13]

In order to discredit India, Pakistan keeps harping on human rights situation in Jammu and Kashmir. This is despite the presence of strong and credible democratic institutions both in Jammu and Kashmir State and at the federal level in India as also complete transparency in every respect ensured by vibrant and free media. India also has a National Human Rights Commission, which thoroughly examines and investigates all complaints of excesses by security forces and punishes those found guilty. It would appear that Pakistan's stance on this score is designed to obscure its own abysmal record on human rights front in the portion of Jammu and Kashmir under its control as is borne out from the draft report of European Parliament on Kashmir, which has castigated Pakistan for failing "to introduce meaningful and representative democratic structures in 'AJK' ('Azad Kashmir')".[14]

The September 2006 report of Human Rights Watch, a well known NGO has described 'Azad Kashmir' as anything but 'Azad'.[15] The report attacked Pakistan for maintaining Pakistan occupied Kashmir, so-called 'Azad Kashmir', as "one of the most closed territories in the world" where Pakistani army and the Pakistani intelligence services (ISI) "control all aspects of political life." It noted that "Azad Kashmir is a land of strict curbs on political pluralism, freedom of expression, and freedom of association; a muzzled press; banned books; arbitrary arrest and detention and torture at the hands of the Pakistani military and the police; and, discrimination against refugees from Jammu and Kashmir state".[16] The report also castigated Pakistan military for maintaining close relations with militant groups in the territory and for even having used the occasion of recent earthquake, which was a massive humanitarian disaster, "as an opportunity to craft a new image for the militant groups rather than as an opportunity to disband them." The report calls upon the international community to insist firmly that Pakistan allows the people of 'Azad Kashmir' to exercise their fundamental civil and political rights "in an environment fire of coercion and fear."[17]

In the Gilgit-Baltistan (termed as the Northern Areas of Pakistan), which were detached from the occupied portion of the J&K state and annexed by Pakistan in the wake of confusion prevailing after Pakistani invasion of J&K in 1947, the situation is far worse. The Northern Areas in PoK suffer from stark poverty and total neglect by Pakistan Government. There is hardly any kind of industry and over 85 per cent of people live below poverty line. The literacy levels are pathetically low, even by the standards of Pakistan. Growing unemployment and almost total drying up of tourism revenue has "created widespread unrest and frustration amongst the masses."[18] Opportunities for higher education are extremely scarce. A university has recently been set up but that does not have the requisite infrastructure. The basic facilities, such as electricity, drinking water and primary health care are virtually non-existent.[19] This region used to be self-sufficient in food but continued neglect by the Pakistani Government and ensuing political crises have left it dependent on outside for most of its essential requirements including food. In recent years even these supplies have been affected due to floods and earthquakes causing untold hardship to people living there.[20]

The territory is administered in effect as a colony and no attempt has been made by the Government of Pakistan to institute any genuine democratic and constitutional mechanism to fulfil people's developmental and political aspirations. Rather, the government has sought to incite sectarian violence in this shia-majority area by way of grafting population from outside.

People living across the line of control in the Pakistani occupied areas of Jammu and Kashmir face grave deprivation and discrimination. They are denied basic amenities of life and do not enjoy any kind of political freedom. Manzoor Hussein Parwana, Chairman of Gilgit-Baltistan United Movement expressing his frustration at "the culture of the gum in the region" has called upon India " to speak up against atrocities committed by the Pakistan army against indigenous people of Gilgit-Baltistan." India has a moral responsibility to inform Indian public and the world at large about the miseries and denial of basic human rights to these people who have been left to be exploited by the oppressive instruments of Pakistani occupation. After all, they are Indians, by virtue of the accession of former J&K State to India in 1947. The fact that the people here look towards India for their salvation was clearly highlighted when they recently lamented that India had not done enough for them and asked for reservation in Indian educational institutions.[21] India, therefore, is duty bound to galvanize the international public opinion to put requisite pressure on Pakistan Government to provide solace to this 'Indian Population'.

This is a broad sketch of the difficulties which India continues to endure on a daily basis in its relations with Pakistan. Given Pakistan's track record of lack of sincerity and active connivance in sponsoring terrorist activities in India, it is only natural for people in India to feel disenchanted with Pakistani leadership and question the advisability of Indian leadership having made yet another overture to Pakistan in Havana. It has been argued, perhaps rightly, that Pakistan can hardly be expected to be the part of the solution if it was itself the

problem in the first place. The disclosure by the Mumbai
Police Chief that the Pakistani intelligence agency ISI was
indeed behind the Mumbai train blasts, as was being suspected
has further aggravated the sense of scepticism in India in
engaging Pakistan any further. The Indian Prime Minister has
rightly asserted that "Pakistan will have to walk the talk." But
that may not have completely assuaged the concerns of people
in India. They will wait to see the ground realities as they
emerge in the coming months and whether the newly created
'Joint Mechanism' proves effective in tackling the problem of
terrorism.

Pakistan needs to realise that the low intensity war that it
is waging against India has absolutely no chance of succeeding
even though it would exact considerable price from both
countries (the cost to Pakistan would always be greater because
of huge asymmetry in the size of the two countries). Pakistan
must also realize that given India's economic and military
wherewithals, no amount of pressure can be brought to bear
on India for it to give up its legitimate and moral claim over
the whole of J&K and to dilute its commitment to ensuring its
territorial integrity. India on its part must also accept that there
can be no military solution to the problem irrespective of how
powerful it becomes. It is pertinent to note that even the most
powerful nation of the world, the USA has found it impossible
to resolve the problems in Iraq to its satisfaction by use of
military force. History, in any case, is replete with examples
to show that military solution alone seldom works. That leaves
only the option of peaceful settlement and it would be unfair
to blame the Indian Government for trying to edge forward
in that direction. India has to give peace all the chance it
deserves and perhaps much more. This is particularly so, since
the people of India do not hold the people of Pakistan
responsible for the past wrong-doings of the successive regimes
in that country. If Mahatma Gandhi were to be alive today he
surely would have given the same advice to the Indians. The
government of India is, therefore, right in pursuing the

Gandhian path and showing the courage to walk the extra mile to pursue peace with Pakistan.

Notes

[1] The word *Dard* was first used by Dr. G.W. Leitner, who cited evidence from Western classical sources and identify *dardae* with *Darada* of Sanskrit writers.

[1] Anand K Verma. *Reassessing Pakistan*. New Delhi: Lancer Publishers & Distributors, 2001, p. 54.

[2] Owen Bennett Jones. *Pakistan Eye of the Storm*. New Delhi: Penguine Books India, 2002, p 113.

[3] Waheguru Pal Singh Sidhu, "Introduction" in Waheguru Pal Singh *et al* edited *Kashmir : New Voices New Approach*. London: Lynne Rienner Publishers, 2006, p 3.

[4] Jasjit Singh, "Pakistan Occupied Kashmir" in Jasjit Singh ed *Pakistan Occupied Kashmir: Under The Jackboot*. New Delhi: Cosmo Publications, 1995, pp 22-24.

[5] Riyaz Punjabi, "India-Pakistan Peace Process: Cautious Optimism", Journal of Peace Studies, Volume 11, Issue 4, October-December 2004, p 84.

[6] Robert G Wirsing, "India-Pakistan Relations and the problem of Kashmir" in Hafeez Malik (ed) *Pakistan: Founders' Aspirations and Today's Realities*. Karachi: Oxford University Press, 2001, p 430.

[7] Owen Benett Jones, no 2 , pp 94-97.

[8] "Musharraf's Kargil account contested by Sartaz Aziz" from Website http://news.indiainfo.com/2006/10/02 0210musharraf-kargil-aziz.html (Accessed on October 15, 2006).

[9] Mary Anne Weaver, *Pakistan: In the Shadow of Jihad and Afghanistan*. New York: Farrar, Straus and Giroux, 2002, p 255.

[10] Ibid, p 252

11   BG Verghese, "A Jammu and Kashmir Primer—From Myth to Reality", Centre for Policy Research Occasional Paper Series, Occasional Paper No 14, p 5.

12   Hafeez Malik, "An Introduction" in Hafeez Malik (ed) *Pakistan: Founders' Aspirations and Today's Realities.* Karachi: Oxford University Press, 2001, pp 10-11.

13   M.L. Kotru, The-Kashmir story, New Delhi: External Publicity Division, Ministry of External Affairs, Government of India, p. 14.

14   Baroness Emma Nicholson of Winterbourne, European Parliament Draft Report on "Kashmir: Present Situation and Future Prospects", dated November 23, 2006, p. 6.

15   Ershad Mahmud, "Azad Kashmir and self-governance", The News October 14, 2006.

16   "With Friends Like These.....", *Human Rights Violations in Azad Kashmir,* Human rights Watch Report, Volume 18, No 12(c), September 2006, pp. 6-7.

17   Ibid., pp. 8-9.

18   Ershad Mahmud. "Challenges Before the New Government in NAs", *The International News* 'Internet Edition' December 11, 2004.

19   "The Northern Areas of Pakistan Occupied Kashmir" from SATP Website http://www.satp.org/sattporgtp/kpsgill/2003/chapter3.htm (Accessed on October 15, 2006).

20   M Ismail Khan, "Avoiding the Highway of Death", The International News, Internet Edition, May 5, 2005.

21   "Northern Areas : A tale of neglect, Denial?" from New Indian Express Website http://www.newindpress.com/NewsItems.asp? ID = IEP20060529092431 & Page = P&Title=Nation&Topic=0 (Accessed on May 30, 2006)

2

Gilgit and Baltistan:
The Historical Dimension

P Stobdan

Pakistan which had recognised the Government of Maharaja of Jammu and Kashmir and concluded a Stand-Still Agreement with it in August 1947, chose to violate all norms of international law by committing an act of aggression against the State three months later. Pakistan blocked the supply of essential commodities. Its nationals and tribal raiders under the guidance and leadership of its army corps invaded the country. Pakistan, however, categorically denied that it had supported the tribal invasion, but it could not hide the truth and justify its presence in Kashmir. It had to disclose to the United Nations Commission for India and Pakistan (UNCIP) in July 1948, that there were three regular Pakistani Brigades fighting in Kashmir territory since May 1948. The two resolutions of the UNCIP (13 August 1948 and 5 January 1949) clearly indicate that the presence of Pakistan in parts of Jammu and Kashmir was illegal, and that it had to withdraw its troops and abandon the aggression against India.

Three major regions, namely, Mirpur-Muzzaffarabad, Gilgit and Baltistan, covering one-third of the total area of 86,023 square miles of the State of Jammu and Kashmir are still under the illegal occupation of Pakistan. What today Pakistan describes as "Northern Areas" include the five districts of Gilgit, Skardu, Diamir, Ghizer and Ghanche covering an area of 72,495 square kilometers with a sparse population of approximately two million.

This chapter attempts to highlight the historical background of Gilgit and Baltistan, their political legacies, conquest by the Sikhs, the Dogra and British rule and their status at the time of Pakistani invasion and after. It also tries to throw light on the current state of affairs in respect of the two regions in the backdrop of Pakistan's dilemma, as well as, the internal political dynamics of the two regions.

GILGIT

The Early History

Gilgit is also known as Dardistan, i.e., the land of the Dards or Dardic speaking people. Dards belong to the Indo-Aryan family of languages.[1] Dards remained *terra incognito* in their early history. They had some association with the protohistoric social groups of Shin and Yashkun. Their appearance in history is related to the movements and migration of the Achamenians, the Scythians, the Kushanas, the Sassanians and the Huns. During 6th to 8th centuries, Gilgit was the home of the Palola or Patola who practised Buddhism and had interactions with the rulers of Kashmir and the emperors of China. The Chinese referred to Gilgit and Baltistan as "Great Bolor" and "Little Bolor" respectively. Apart from Chinese and Kashmiri influence, the Tibetans also managed to hold sway in the area particularly in Baltistan. The medieval history of the region is linked to the ruling families[2] firstly from Hunza, Nagar, Punial, Yasin, Ghizer and Chitral, and the second lineage belonging to the ruling families from Skardu, Khapalu, Shigar, Rondu, Astor, Karatshe, Tolti, Kargil and Dras. Baltistan is being dealt separately in this chapter.

Although very little is known about the political formations in Gilgit in ancient times, historians talk about a local ruler of

The State of Jammu & Kashmir

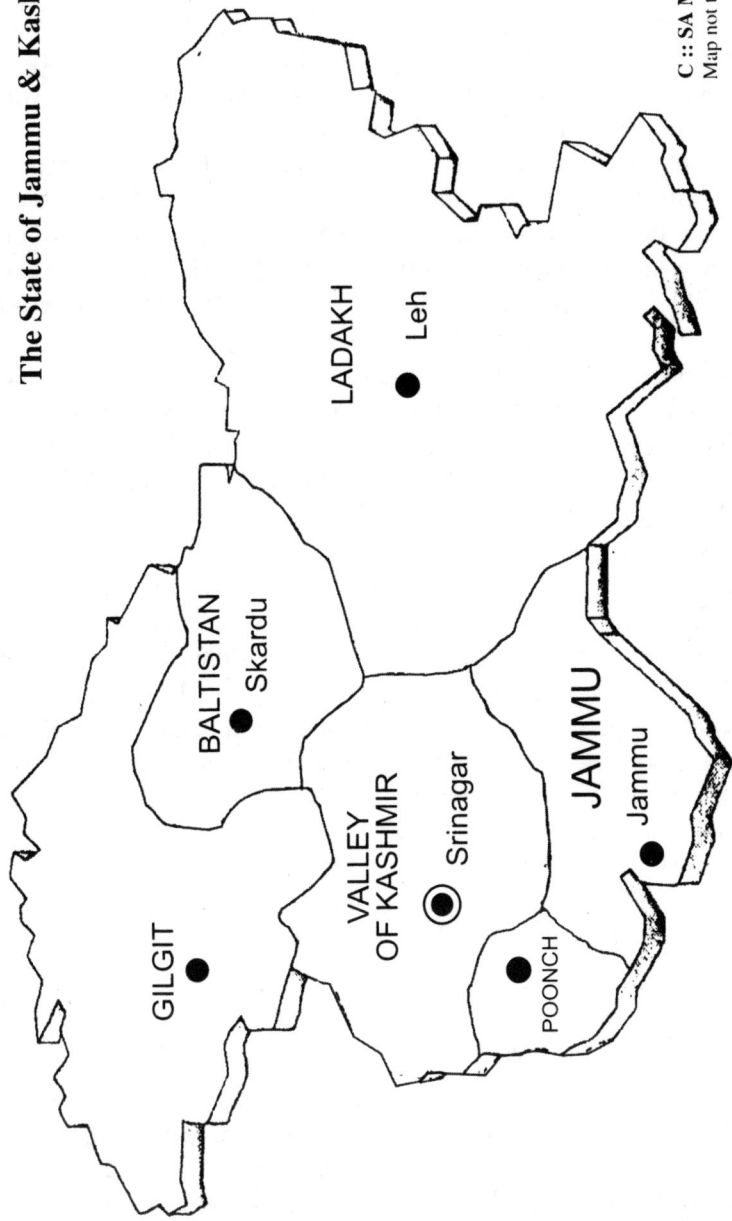

C :: **SA Mac**
Map not to scale

Gilgit by the name of Agartham sometime in the 8th century[3]. He is said to have been defeated by Abudgamo from Baltistan in the year 750. Abudgamo founded the Shah Rais dynasty in Gilgit. He was succeeded by his son Sri Bagatham who was a follower of Buddhism. After several generations Sri Badat occupied the throne around the period 1080 who patronised Buddhism and built many *Viharas* in Gilgit, Punial and Yasin. He was the last Buddhist ruler when Hunza ruler Shamsher, a Muslim, killed Badat around 1120. Shamsher founded the Tarakhan dynasty in Gilgit and ruled up to 1160. He patronised Islam in Gilgit and built many mosques in the region. It was during his rule that the poorer sections of society — the Dooms, the Kamins and the Yashkuns were converted to Islam. The reign of Tarakhan dynasty came to an end around 1335 with the invasion of Gilgit by Taj Mughal of Badakhshan. Taj Mughal introduced the *Ismailia* doctrines whose followers now comprise the Molai sect. Taj Mughal's religious interest reached up to Kashgar. Gilgit faced successive invasions from the neighbouring Rajas, and during the 18th century Gilgit was ruled by Mohammed Khan, who was defeated by Sulaiman Shah, the ruler of Yasin who ruled Gilgit till 1828. Sulaiman Khan was later killed by Punial ruler Azad Khan. Azad Khan was killed by Raja of Nagar, Tahir Khan. He ruled Gilgit till 1837. He was succeeded by his son Shah Sikander. He was killed by Gaur Rehman, ruler of Yasin. Gaur Rehman became the last ruler of Gilgit in the year 1841. Earlier Shah Sikander's brother Karim Khan, having escaped from Gaur, sent an agent to the Sikh Governor of Kashmir imploring aid against the invader.

The Sikh Conquest

In 1842, in order to help Karim Khan, brother of Sikander Khan, the Sikh Governor of Kashmir sent troops to Gilgit under the leadership of Nathu Shah and Mathra Dass. The Dogra troops helped Karim Khan defeat Gaur Rehman who fled to Punial. Nathu Shah, however, remained there and married the daughter of Gaur Rehman to himself and the daughters of Hunza and Nagar to his sons. Karim Khan was made the titular Raja of Gilgit in the name of Sikh Government; a small Sikh force was stationed at Gilgit under a Thanedar. Nathu Shah later returned to Srinagar to transfer his power to the new ruler of Kashmir Maharaja Gulab Singh who had concluded the Treaty of Amritsar in 1846 with the British Government and secured political control over Kashmir including the areas around Gilgit.

The Dogra Rule

Kashmir along with Gilgit was ceded to Gulab Singh in 1846. Nathu Shah left for Gilgit with two Europeans but the ruler of Hunza killed him together with Karim Khan for bringing two foreigners to the frontier. Gaur Rehman, the ruler of Punial and Yasin joined him against the Dogras. The people of Darel also joined Gaur Rehman, who captured Gilgit again.

Maharaja Gulab Singh died in 1857. His son, Ranbir Singh soon after his ascension to the throne, dispatched a large force to Gilgit under General Devi Singh. Not only did the Dogra force conquer Gilgit but it also captured Yasin and Punial and made Uzmat Shah and Isa Bahadur Governors of the two regions. Chilas and Darel were conquered in 1851 and 1866 respectively. The tribals showed their resentment of Dogra rule at every opportunity. The rulers of Hunza and Nagar also became tributaries of the Kashmir State, but they too often gave trouble to Maharaja's garrison at Gilgit.

Gilgit Agency

The British Government recognised Maharaja Gulab Singh's full "independence" over Kashmir and its neighbouring territories as per the 1846 Treaty of Amritsar, but it always sought to interfere or at times chose to re-interpret the contents of this "independence". The British interference was in general necessitated by the Russian expansion in Central Asia, perceived as a great threat to the empire's wider strategic interests. However, there were other considerations too. British interference in Kashmir's internal affairs was mostly under the pretext of the severe hardships the Maharaja inflicted on the people.

Having annexed Punjab, the British were attracted towards Kashmir for commercial exploitation of the fine and costly products of Kashmiri looms (shawl), the potential and climatical suitability of Kashmir for a great Missionary Centre for the vast countries of Tibet, China, Yarkand, Afghanistan and Turkistan. Not surprisingly, many Britishers began to admire the beauty of Kashmir. E.F. Knight thought that "The climate of this paradise of Asia appears to be well adapted to the European constitution", but he simultaneously also regretted the sale of this beautiful valley to the Maharaja: "Had we not sold this magnificent country, a great military cantonment would no doubt have long since been established here. This would not only have been most advantageous from a strategic point of view but would have avoided much of the sickness and mortality which thin the ranks of our white army in India."[4] A similar viewpoint was also expressed by Brinkman — "If properly ruled Cashmere would pay us ten times over, and far more than any other spot in India does. The country would pay as a sanitorium the force to keep it in order...."[5]

Political upheavals in North India, following the 1857 Mutiny shocked the British. The Maharaja of Kashmir offered military and material help to the British to suppress the insurrection. In return, Lord Canning, the Viceroy, gladly issued a *sanad* as *quid pro quo* providing Ranbir Singh the right to adopt an heir for him and his successors to perpetuate their dynastic rule. The promise, however, was not kept by the British. They, later on, suitably modified their demand of annexation, as *Delhi Gazette* observed — " We do not advocate annexation but we do affirm that a military occupation of Cashmere has now become in our self-defence, actual necessity."

The British strategic calculations began to change later in the backdrop of Russian expansion in Central Asia in mid-1860s. The British persuaded Maharaja Ranbir Singh and expressed desire that "States such as Chitral and Yasin should come under the control of a friend and an ally of the British Government like His Highness, rather than be absorbed in the course of events by powers inimical to Kashmir." Gilgit Agency was set up in 1877 with the appointment of Major John Biddulph as the first Political Agent. The Agent was withdrawn in 1881 because of a new foothold in Jalalabad, but it was re-established in 1889 in the wake of increasing Afghan intrigue in Chitral, as well as, Russia's military activities in Central Asia. The importance of Gilgit, for the British is reflected in E.F. Knight's words.

> "The value of Gilgit to Kashmir State, commanding as it does the Indus Valley and the mouth of the Hunza river, and so holding in check the unruly tribes on either side, is obvious enough; but it is only recently that the great strategical importance to the empire of this position has been fully realised....Whatever position we take up with regard to the debatable land beyond Hindukush there can be no doubt as to what our course of action should be on the southern slope.... It is necessary for the safeguarding of our Empire that we should at any rate hold our side of the mountain gates but unless we locked it in, Russia would soon have both sides under her control."[6]

Towards the end of the century the Strategic Committee of the Government of India not only succeeded in getting constructed a road to Srinagar but also recommended its extension up to Gilgit and Chitral. The confidential reports and recommendations prepared by Colonel Lockhart, the Deputy Quarter-Master General after his Gilgit Mission, further helped the Government consolidate its control over Gilgit and adjoining areas.

By 1891, Hunza and Nagar were subjugated under the leadership of Colonel Durand. The British managed to bring the entire region of Gilgit under Government of India's control. Appointment of Colonel Durand at Gilgit marked the re-establishment of the British Agency. He established direct political relationship with the local rulers.They professed unbounded loyalty to the British Government. As Dr Arthur Neve wrote:

> "To the Englishman the word Gilgit should recall the many gallant deeds of the nineties—the capture of Hunza, the relief of Chitral and the Pamir Commission. During the last half century Kashmir is the only Indian native State that has increased in area. And the increase was not desired but was forced upon the Imperial Government by the advancing power of the Russian Empire and the intrigues of its frontier officers."[7]

Lord Curzon underlined the strategic importance of Gilgit to India in the words:

> "it is one of the northern gates of India, through which a would-be invader must advance, if he advances at all. Gilgit occupies a strategic place and the Indian Government, harassed by Russia's growing restlessness in Central Asia, knew it for the key of great northern gateway into India, a key worth holding even at some cost in toil, money and valuable though less — human lives."[8]

The importance of British control of the Gilgit Agency was stated by Colonel Durand:

> "—why it has been asked should it be worth our while to interfere there with whatever happened? The answer is of course Russia — expensive as the Gilgit game might have been, it was worth the candle."[9]

Having reorganised the military and civil administration of the Agency in Gilgit, the British Government began to treat these frontier States not as part of the territories of the Jammu and Kashmir State, though the rulers of all these States accepted the Maharaja as their suzerain. In 1900, the rulers of Hunza, Nagar and Punial were invited to Calcutta, as guests of the Viceroy.

In 1901, the combined *Wazarat* of the Frontier District was recognised into two *Wazarats* of Gilgit and Ladakh. Gilgit *Wazarat* comprised Gilgit and Astor *Tehsils* and the *Niabat* at Bunji. The State Government had control over only the *Wazarat.* The Political Agent controlled remaining districts of the Gilgit Agency. Similarly, Chitral, Hunza and Nagar though under the Maharaja's suzerainty, were directly under the control of Political Agent. The British policy towards these small States was to allow the local rulers to govern themselves, without much interference from the State Government.

In view of the course of affairs on the Afghan frontier that increased the prospects of war between England and Russia, the Princely States in India offered to place all their resources at the disposal of the British Government. The Maharaja of Kashmir also agreed to contribute to the defence of the Empire. In 1889, the "Kashmir Imperial Service Troops" was organised, trained by the British and placed under an English officer, Col.Neville Chamberlain, appointed by the Jammu and Kashmir State as its Military Secretary. By 1900, the entire military administration in Gilgit and other tribal areas of the Kashmir State was brought under the British control.

With the abolition of the Military Levies in 1913, a new force was organised under the name of Gilgit Scouts who were responsible for both internal and external defence. After the withdrawal of the Kashmir Imperial Service Troops in 1935, the Gilgit Scouts became entirely responsible for the defence and internal security of the Gilgit Agency.

The British Government deposed Maharaja Pratap Singh levelling several charges against him, including those of tyranny and misrule. The issue became a subject of debate in the British Parliament and media and remained so for several decades. It is not necessary here to go into details, but it would be appropriate here to say that the British Government violated the Treaty of 1846, by appointing a Resident in Kashmir and gradually deposing the Maharaja through the system of levelling charges on the basis of forged letters and rumours. The British Government had no right to send a Resident to Kashmir, because the State was not included amongst the feudatory until 1885. In virtually deposing Maharaja Pratap Singh, the British were really activated by strategic concerns, and the apprehension of Russian expansion.

The British favoured Hari Singh, the son of Raja Amar Singh, as successor to the throne. This was in spite of the wishes to the contrary of Maharaja Pratap Singh. By this stratagem, the Resident became *de facto* ruler of Kashmir from 1889 to 1921 and took care of the imperial interests at the cost of the interests of the people of the State. Hari Singh, however, did not approve of the imperial ambitions and started asserting his right to control up to Gilgit. He objected to the flying of the Union Jack which was being furled wherever the British liked. He replaced the Union Jack with the State flag in Gilgit and other buildings in Kashmir. Administration was tightened in Gilgit. Hari Singh vigorously pursued the process of "hereditary state subject" with legal precision.

Except for Gilgit *Wazarat* which was ruled by Kashmir *Darbar,* the other areas of Gilgit were only suzerainties of Kashmir State. They were not treated as territories of Kashmir. The British allowed the local people to govern themselves, according to their customary laws and customs.

Lease of Gilgit

Russian threat to the northern frontier of India had been seriously taken into account by the British since the days of Lord Curzon. The October 1917 Revolution increased the

British anxieties over Russian moves. Aware of possible repercussions in Kashmir also, the Maharaja agreed to lease the Gilgit Agency to the British following an agreement signed on March 26,1935. (See Appendix I)

Article 1 of the Agreement gave the Viceroy and Governor General of India the right "to assume the civil and military administration of so much of the *Wazarat* of Gilgit Province of the State of Jammu and Kashmir, as lies beyond the right bank of the river Indus". The Maharaja could not resist the British pressure in view of the rising tide of people's movement in the State.

The status and relationships of these areas with the Agency and the Kashmir State prior to the lease of Gilgit Agency to the British in 1935 were :

1. The Gilgit Wazarat

It comprised the Tehsils of Gilgit and Astor and the Niabat of Bunji. It was under the direct control of the Kashmir Darbar. The Officer was called *Wazir-i-Wazarat.*

2. Hunza and Nagar

Hunza and Nagar were referred to as States. After a military operation against the State of Hunza and Nagar in 1891, the Maharaja of Kashmir with the approval and authority of the Governor-General-in-Council, installed Muhammad Nazim Khan as ruler of Hunza. A *Sanad* was issued by the Maharaja to the ruler that the Chieftainship of the Hunza State would be hereditary of his family. He was assured protection so long as his family remained loyal to the State of Jammu and Kashmir and to the British Government. An annual tribute of 25 tilloos of gold, equal to 16 *tolas* and 5 *mashas* to be paid to the State of Jammu and Kashmir was fixed.

Similar *Sanad* was issued to the *Mir* of Nagar, Jaffa Khan. An annual tribute of 26 tilloos of gold equal to 17 *tolas* and 1 *masha* was fixed.

Both Hunza and Nagar were given subsidies of Rs 4,000 each year.

3. Chitral

The ruler of the Chitral was called Mehtar. Chitral acknowledged the suzerainty of the Maharaja of Kashmir, and through him of the British Government in 1878. Unlike other vassal States, Chitral continued its allegiance to the Maharaja and the British Government until 1947. The Mehtar of Chitral enjoyed the title of "His Highness" and the right of having a salute of 11 guns.

4. Punial

The district of Punial came under the possession of the Maharaja in 1860. Raja Isa Bahadur was made the local ruler. The Raja of Punial was known for his loyalty to the Maharaja and the British Government. The ruler received a subsidy of Rs. 1,200 a year which was fixed in 1895. In 1927, it was increased to Rs.1,600 paid by the Government of India. Punial did not pay tribute to the Kashmir Darbar.

5. Yasin and Kuh-Ghizer

In 1895, Yasin was separated from the Chitral State and brought under the Governorship of the Gilgit Agency. Mehtarjao Abdur Rehman Khan was appointed to the Governorship of Yasin in 1895 by the Political Agent in the name of the Maharaja of Kashmir. In 1905 Kuh-Ghizer was incorporated under the Governorship of Yasin. Later it was separated into two Governorships. The Governors paid part of their revenue to the Kashmir Darbar. Both the Governors received Rs. 1,200 annually from Kashmir Darbar as subsidy.

6. Ish Kaman

Ish Kaman was also separated from Chitral and placed under a Governorship — a paid official without any hereditary claims. Mir Ali Mardan Shah was first the Governor of Ish Kaman. His terms and conditions were same as those of Kuh-Ghizer and Yasin.

7. Chilas

Chilas was occupied in 1893, and was placed in the charge of a political officer called Assistant Political Agent, Chilas. Chilas paid an annual tribute of Rs. 3,000 to Kashmir. Because of the distance and hardship, Chilas was allowed to pay the tribute to Kashmir Darbar every third year.

8. Gor

Gor enjoyed special privileges due to their uninterrupted help to the British. Gor paid tribute to Kashmir, through the *Wazir-i-Wazarat* in Gilgit.

9. Darel and Tangir

Darel and Tangir were small, separate, semi-independent states and had accepted the suzerainty of Kashmir. They used to cause much trouble to the Gilgit Agency and were effectively brought under control by the British.

BALTISTAN

The Early History

Baltistan, the land of Balti people, was well known as "Little Tibet" or *Tibet-i-Khurd* in the medieval literature. Early history of Baltistan begins with spread of Buddhism under the Kushanas. Tibetans were also active from the 8th century. Except for a few Tibetan inscriptions there is no evidence that Baltistan was under the Tibetan State control till the end of 9th century. Later history suggests that large number of immigrants from Kashmir and the other areas penetrated Baltistan and perhaps ruled the State.

In the beginning of the 13th century, an adventurer called Ibrahim Shah founded the Makpon dynasty in Baltistan. Some historians consider Ibrahim a Kashmiri,[10] while others trace his origins to Egypt. Ibrahim married a local princess and laid the foundation of a new dynasty. Around the 15th century, when Skardu was ruled by Makpon Bokha, a Muslim missionary

Mir Shamsuddin Iraqi is believed to have reached Baltistan to spread Islam. Other historians believe that Mohammed Nur Bakhsh, the founder of the Nurbakhshi order came to Baltistan to spread Islam in 1448.[11]

Makpon Bokha is said to have founded the State of Baltistan in about 15th century. He also made an administrative seat and palace at Kharpoche and built a fort there. He allowed Mir Shamsuddin Iraqi to preach Islam. Bokha also patronised craftsmen from Chilas and Kashmir and kept commercial relations with Yarkand, Kashgar, Hunza, Nagar, Gilgit and Kashmir.

The Balti State fought a number of wars with the neighbouring States. Towards the end of the 15th century the boundary between Baltistan and Ladakh was fixed by Ali Sher Khan who was then the ruler of the Balti State. Ali Sher Khan later extended his rule up to Dardistan. He defeated many kings of Gilgit and Chitral. His extensive conquests earned him the title of *Anchaî Azam*. The successors of Ali Sher Khan fought among themselves. Internecine wars also followed with the neighbouring smaller kingdoms, until the Balti State fell under the suzerainty of the Mughal emperors during the reigns of Shah Jahan and Aurangzeb. Later, during the period of decline of the Mughals and ascendancy of Afghans in Kashmir, Baltis regained control over their State. Prior to the rise of the Sikh rule, Baltistan witnessed great turmoil mainly because of the fighting among various local chieftains and wars with the Gyalpos of Ladakh. The most powerful of all of them in 1840 was the Raja of Skardu, Ahmed Shah to whom others owed fealty.

The Dogra Conquest

After conquering Ladakh in 1836, the Dogras turned towards Baltistan. That they could make it the next target and succeed in conquering it easily was also due to the continuous dissensions and unrest prevailing among the Baltis. In Skardu, Ahmed Shah and his eldest son Mohammed Shah were seriously estranged. The Dogras were also provoked by Balti efforts to cultivate friendship with the British and seek protection from them against the possible invasion by the Dogra troops. In 1839,[12] Zorawar Singh, the Dogra General led an army of 15,000 Dogras and a Ladakhi contingent to conquer Baltistan. Ahmed Shah of Skardu surrendered to the Dogras in 1840. Zorawar Singh installed Mohammed Shah as a puppet ruler, who agreed to pay seven thousand rupees to Jammu.[13] Zorawar Singh later stationed a garrison of Dogra troops at Skardu and returned to Leh, the capital of Ladakh. Thus Baltistan became part of Ladakh province of the Jammu Maharaja's kingdom much before Kashmir and Gilgit became part of it. The Dogras had direct control over Skardu and Leh. However, Pakistani invaders extended themselves into large parts of Baltistan essentially between August 1948, when the India-Pakistan ceasefire was accepted and December 31,1948 when it came into effect. India now has about 2,000 square miles, comprising present Kargil district, out of the total area of 14,000 square miles of Baltistan.

POLITICAL STATUS IN 1947-1948

With the termination of the 1935 lease and the lapse of paramountcy, the entire area of Gilgit *Wazarat* and Gilgit Agency was restored under the control of the Maharaja of Kashmir. The Gilgit *Wazarat* was returned completely as before, the Gilgit Agency, along with the direct relationship with Mirs and Rajas concerned.

Prior to the lease, the Gilgit *Wazarat* enjoyed the same status as other *Wazarats in* the State. In view of the lapse of paramountcy and its strategic importance, the State Government decided to bring about certain administrative changes to treat Gilgit as a Governor's province, naming it the Frontier Province. It also took over the entire Gilgit Scouts Force and other employees. Accordingly, Brigadier Ghansar Singh was deputed by Maharaja as Governor of these areas.

He took over charge from the Political Agent Lt Colonel Beacon on August 1, 1947.

The Governor accompanied by the Chief of Staff, General Scott met the officers and (JCOs) of the Gilgit Scouts and was handed over a series of demands relating to the service conditions. They promised to serve the State if their demands were met.

The local Rajas welcomed the return of Maharaja's rule but the Gilgit Scouts led by Major Brown continued to defy the Governor. Brigadier Ghansar Singh writes in "Gilgit Before 1947" that the general impression was that the British Officers did not like this change although the common man was pleased with it. On October 31, 1947, Gilgit Scouts surrounded his house and demanded his surrender. The Governor was arrested and imprisoned. The Pakistani propaganda apparently played on the religious sentiments of the Muslim soldiers in Maharaja's army and in Gilgit Scouts to incite them to revolt and detach the region from the rest of Kashmir. Later events like Pakistan's inclusion in western defence pacts indicate that the revolt in northern territory could have been politically motivated by the British officers to keep it under the control of a trusted power — Pakistan.

It must be noted that neither the local Mirs and Rajas, nor the people of the area over whom the Maharaja had full authority, were in any way involved in any armed rebellion, which was the handiwork of a military junta. Except in the case of Mehtar of Chitral, the Maharaja enjoyed the full support from Mirs of Hunza, Nagar and Raja of Punial. In fact the Raja of Punial came to help Ghansar Singh, the Governor, along with his bodyguards. Most of the local rulers decided to accept the will of the Maharaja whatever he decides i.e., either to join Pakistan or to go to India. There was no question of people's participation as there was no political party or organisation in the area.

After occupying Gilgit the rebels captured Baltistan in the East. For 17 days these areas were known as "People's Republic of Gilgit and Baltistan", under a provisional Government, formed by the rebels and headed by one local Rais Khan. Major Brown hoisted the Pakistani flag in Gilgit on November 4, 1947. Pakistani authorities in Peshawar were asked to send Political Agent to rule over this area. Pakistan sent Sardar Mohammad Alam as its first political agent. Pakistan made this transfer formal by signing an agreement with the Presidents of "Azad Kashmir" and the Muslim Conference on April 28, 1949. Under this agreement the Government of Pakistan secured legitimacy of sorts to keep Gilgit and Baltistan under its administrative control.

STATUS OF SHAKSGAM-MUZTAGH VALLEY
Area ceded to China

The Hunza and Nagar States came under British occupation in 1891-92. The rulers of these States paid tribute to the State of Jammu and Kashmir. Problems in this area were linked with claims of the Mir of Hunza to the outlying grazing grounds around the watershed demarcation. Many of the forward alignments in this area had in fact appeared on British maps. The Chinese always maintained in the past that they never had any direct administration in Hunza, and admitted the existence of a boundary of some kind between Hunza and Chinese Turkistan.[14] However, Communist China produced a map in 1959 which included some 6,000 square miles in the Hunza and Gilgit area as Chinese.[15] The Chinese also made military intrusions in the area in 1953.

Pakistan after occupying the area of Gilgit and adjoining tributary States of Kashmir in 1948, made its first move to settle the boundaries with China in January 1961. Earlier the Chinese had refused to discuss any part of the frontier West of Karakoram Pass in the official Sino-Indian meetings. Beijing's first response to Pakistani proposal came in February 1962; and in May 1962, Beijing announced officially that the Government of China and Pakistan have agreed to negotiate on the boundary-question. In a joint communique it was added that resulting settlement would be provisional, pending a solution of the dispute over Kashmir between India and Pakistan. On March 2, 1963, Sino-Pakistan frontier agreement was signed in Beijing by Pakistani Foreign Minister Bhutto and Chinese Foreign Minister Chen Yi.

India expressed concern over the agreement and protested against this illegal demarcation of India's frontier with China. India's Defence Minister Krishna Menon in the United Nation Security Council in May and June 1962 said:

"Over and above all this then has occurred the situation in which Pakistan today — not for any good reason, but merely for nuisance value and as an instrument to put pressure on us — has entered into negotiations and, I believe, has concluded agreements with the Central Government of the People's Republic of China. That agreement is in total violation of any rights or authority Pakistan may possess, for Pakistan has no sovereignty over this State; it is not Pakistan's to trade away or to negotiate about. Secondly, it was not necessary even for considerations relating to Pakistan's own security. What is more, it has been done on a basis which we cannot accept — that is to say, our position in regard to China and Chinese claims, which is not under discussion before the Security Council".[16]

The Government of India also sent protest notes to China and Pakistan on May 10, 1962, stating *inter alia:*

"In lodging an emphatic protest with the government of the People's Republic of China for this interference with the sovereignty of India over the State of Jammu and Kashmir, the Government of India solemnly warns the Government of China that any change, provisional or otherwise, in the status of the state of Jammu and Kashmir brought about by third parties which seek to submit certain parts of Indian territory to foreign jurisdiction will not be binding on the Government of India and that the Government of India firmly repudiate any agreements, provisional or otherwise, regarding her own territories arrived at between third parties who have no legal or constitutional *locus standi* of any kind.

It is clear that the Government of China are in this matter acting in furtherance of their aggressive designs and are seeking to exploit the troubled situation in Kashmir and India's differences with

Pakistan for their advantage. The Government of India will hold the Government of China responsible for the consequences of their action."[17]

The Chinese, however, replied on May 31, 1962 to state that:[18]

"More than ten years have passed and despite the best wishes and expectations all along cherished by China, this dispute between India and Pakistan remains unsettled. In this circumstance, any one with common sense can understand that the Chinese Government can not leave unsettled indefinitely its boundary of several hundred kilometers with the areas the defence of which is under the control of Pakistan merely because there is a dispute between India and Pakistan over Kashmir. It is entirely necessary, proper, legitimate, and in accordance with international practice for the Chinese Government to agree with the Government of Pakistan to negotiate a provisional agreement concerning this boundary pending a final settlement of the Kashmir question. What fault can be found with this?

Pakistan too stated that India has no right to question the right of Pakistan to enter into negotiations with China to reach an understanding on the alignment of that portion of the territory for the defence of which Pakistan is responsible.

Following the agreement Pakistan claimed that it had gained an area of 750 square miles out of the agreement. Pakistani sources gave the following estimate figure:[19]

Area in previous dispute	3,400 sq. miles
Agreed as China's territory	2,050 sq. miles
(Shaksgam-Muztagh valley Area)	
Agreed as Pakistan's territory (including 750 sq.miles which had been under Chinese control)	1,350 sq. miles

India, however, accused Pakistan for ceding to China about 2,700 sq.miles of Shaksgam and Muztagh Valley of the State of Jammu and Kashmir.

Conclusion

Ever since Pakistan illegally occupied parts of Jammu and Kashmir State which had acceded to India, it has attempted to reorganise the former administration areas. It fiddled with the historical and political aspects of the units of the State in order to create confusion and then annex the occupied area into its own. What Pakistan called "Northern Area" are the former Gilgit Agency, Gilgit *Wazarat,* Astor *Wazarat and Skardu Tehsil of* Ladakh *Wazarat.*

Until the Jammu and Kashmir's interim constitution was promulgated in 1974, relations between Pakistan and occupied territories were guided by the so-called Karachi Agreement of 1949, signed between Pakistan government and President of Muslim Conference, wherein the matters such as defence, foreign affairs (including UN negotiation) and administration of Gilgit and Baltistan were left with Pakistan Government. Among other reasons there was also the relative inaccessibility of Gilgit and Baltistan. This agreement was supposed to have been a temporary 'agreement, in view of the fact that a plebiscite would soon take place.

This was done with the understanding that Pakistan would administer Gilgit and Baltistan as a delegation of the authority vested in the Jammu and Kashmir Government. On several occasions Pakistan could not but mention that these territories are part of the   State of Jammu and Kashmir. In the first instance, the commission issued to the JCOs of the Gilgit Scouts (later converted to the Northern Light Infantry) were in the name of President of "Azad Jammu and Kashmir" ('AJK') rather than the President of Pakistan. Secondly, Pakistan is committed to its stand at the UN, that Gilgit and Baltistan are part of the plebiscite areas. Thirdly, Pakistan agreed in the

Sino-Pakistan Frontier Agreement of 1963 that the sovereignty of this area did not rest with Pakistan, and once the Kashmir dispute is resolved the boundary treaty could be renegotiated.

Having acknowledged at various occasions Gilgit and Baltistan as parts of the State of Jammu and Kashmir, Pakistan has also been taking contradictory stand that Gilgit and Baltistan belonged to Pakistan, because the people of the region liberated themselves from Srinagar and joined Pakistan. There is no doubt that the people of the region have so far strongly resisted their absorption into Pakistan, nor have they preferred to join the so called "Azad Kashmir" ('AJK'), which in any case is not the sole successor of the State of Jammu and Kashmir. The legal developments which took place in Pakistan also suggest that Gilgit and Baltistan could not be incorporated into Pakistan's constitution (Article 1), nor the so-called 'AJK' Interim Constitution promulgated in 1974 defined these areas as under its administrative control.

The people of Gilgit and Baltistan have been subjected to a variety of atrocities and discrimination under the Pakistani rule. Since its occupation Gilgit and Baltistan have been controlled directly by the Ministry of Kashmir Affairs in Islamabad. The Federal Government directly exercises the powers of a provisional Government through the Resident Commissioner, who is an outsider equivalent to a colonial Governor.

There have been a series of developments in Pakistan and in 'AJK' which are aimed at absorbing Gilgit and Baltistan into their respective jurisdiction. Starting from the time of Zia-ul-Haq regime, efforts were being made to find a solution to the status of Gilgit and Baltistan. There have been debates in Pakistan over Gilgit and Baltistan becoming the fifth province of the Federation. The accession of Gilgit and Baltistan could be possible through an Act of Parliament and by constitutional amendment. However, Islamabad is confronted, apart from objection of 'AJK', with three major obstacles in the act of incorporation. Firstly, it requires the consent of other provinces to create a province of Gilgit and Baltistan by creating National Assembly Seats and Senators. Secondly, Islamabad is faced with the problem created by its own stand on Kashmir. Absorption of Gilgit and Baltistan would mean Pakistan acknowledging India's right to hold the territories of Jammu and Kashmir. Thirdly, of course, the people of Gilgit and Baltistan demand separate entity to themselves.

Pakistanis at various points of time have shown enthusiasm about absorption of Gilgit and Baltistan as part of deal brokered by the US for the final solution of Kashmir problem.

In 1993, the "Azad Jammu and Kashmir" High Court had declared that Gilgit and Baltistan (Gilgit, Baltistan etc.) are legally part of Kashmir and should be reverted to the 'AJK', The AJK's stand is same as that of India. It claims that Gilgit and Baltistan were ruled by the Dogra Maharaja. The British had extracted the region from the Dogras on lease but never actually removed it from the ownership of the Maharaja. The lease had reverted after the British left. Within Pakistani framework, the 'AJK' has all the legal rights to reclaim Gilgit and Baltistan. However, four decades of separation has created certain technical problems which may go against the reunion of Gilgit and Baltistan into the 'AJK'. Firstly, it is privately felt by the leading politicians of 'AJK' that inclusion of Gilgit and Baltistan would mean increasing the number of seats in Legislative Assembly by at least a quarter which will upset the political balance in the AJK. Secondly, its merger will create administrative problems particularly due to the inaccessibility of the region. Thirdly, the re-incorporation of Gilgit and Baltistan into the AJK may lead to sectarian clashes. Already, the sectarian conflicts have become the core political issue and·cause of secessionist movement in Baltistan.

The Pakistanis also talk of various options regarding the status of Gilgit and Baltistan. One option talked of is the granting of a Legislature with a Chief Minister, as well as, a High Court of its own to the region. Whereas, it could have a common President and a Supreme Court with the 'AJK', combined with representation for Gilgit and Baltistan on the 'AJK' Council (which functions both as an Upper House for the 'AJK' legislature, as well as an interface for the Pakistan and 'AJK'). Such a mechanism according to the Pakistan would qualify the status of Gilgit and Baltistan as a part of 'AJK' until the UN plebiscite and at the same time it will ensure the local demand for autonomy.

The administration of Gilgit and Baltistan has been directly run by the Ministry of Kashmir, which itself has developed a vested interest to resist any change in the present set-up. After six decades of Pakistani double talk over the status of Gilgit and Baltistan, it cannot even support the independence of the State of Jammu and Kashmir, for fear of losing Gilgit and Baltistan.

The Pakistani Government had announced a package of "reforms", both administrative and judicial, for Gilgit and Baltistan which allowed the people of Gilgit and Baltistan the semblance of a vote for the first time in 1994. This came about in view of the ongoing protest by the people against the Government for discrimination and neglect of the region since the time of its illegal occupation by Pakistan in 1947.

The reforms package was expected to increase the strength of the then existing Northern Area Council from 18 to 26. However, the Chairman of the Council continued to be the Pakistani Minister, for Kashmir and Northern areas. Islamabad's move had been perceived by many people in the POK as a camouflage for its questionable intentions. They had accused the Benazir Government of sending senior officials from North West Frontier Province (NWFP) to senior administrative posts in Gilgit and Baltistan to prepare the ground for the final act of its incorporation in Pakistan's NWFP.

Unlike the semi-autonomous "Azad Kashmir" Government, Gilgit and Baltistan are directly governed by a federal Ministry which exercises the powers of the provisional Government for Gilgit and Baltistan. In 1993 the President of Pakistan Ishaq Khan had dissolved all elected institutions in Gilgit and Baltistan, which engendered protests in the region. It was also alleged that the then Federal Minister in charge of the areas had got the council and other elective bodies filled with his men through one-sided election.

The entire question of Gilgit-Baltistan is a complex one even within Pakistan. As it has been mentioned earlier, people of the region belong to different ethnic groups, within which there are diverse sub-ethnic communities practising different sects of Islam. The major social divisions are along caste lines — Yashkun, Shin, Ronu, Kremin and Doom. Yashkuns form an overwhelming majority, followed by Shins. The people of Baltistan are altogether a different race. They belong to the Tibeto-Mongoloid stock. Majority of people follow either Molai or Shia sects, and only few follow Sunnism. Sectarianism is a serious problem which weakens the regional identity of Gilgit and Baltistan.

The people of the 'AJK' generally talk of their sentimental attachment with the people of Gilgit and Baltistan. But the feeling is not reciprocated. The only commonality among the Kashmiris and the people of Gilgit and Baltistan is that they were all ruled by the Dogras.

Islamisation of Pakistan under General Zia resulted in the emergence of organisation like the *Tehrik Nifas Figh Jafaria* to protect the interests of Shia minority in Pakistan. This, in turn led to the formation of the *Anjuman Sipah Sahaba* (ASSP) to voice the sectarian rhetoric of Sunni majority. Besides, there are numerous other sectarian organisations, which came up during Zia's regime. These organisations are further sustained with the help of sources outside Pakistan. In Gilgit and Baltistan too,, Pakistan always tried to divide the people along the sectarian lines. During Zia's martial law period, not only *Molaism* gained popularity but also Shariat law was introduced in the name of Islam. Besides, the Iranians and the Saudis have also promoted their variant of Shia and Wahabi movements. Gilgit has been witnessing large scale sectarian clashes since 1982 following the assassination of the leaders of the two different communities. While the region's population is divided — Sunnis for integration with POK and Shias for upholding the regional identity, there is little for Pakistan to achieve for itself in Gilgit and Baltistan. Under the circumstances the so-called 'Northern Areas' of the Jammu and Kashmir State should either be an independent State or part of the territories which acceded to India in 1947.

Appendix I

Lease of Gilgit

Agreement between the British Government and Colonel His Highness Maharaja Hari Singh. Inder Mohinder Bahadur, G.C.S.I, G.C.I.E., K.C.V.O., A.D.C., Maharaja of Jammu and Kashmir, his heirs and successors, executed on the one part by Lieutenant Colonel Lionel Edward Lang, C.I.E., M.C., in virtue of full powers vested in him by His Excellency the Right Honourable Freeman Thomas, Earl of Willingdon. P.C, G.M.S.I., G.C.M.G., G.M.I.E., O.B.E., Viceroy and Governor-General of India, and on the other part by Colonel His Highness Maharaja Hari Singh aforesaid. It is hereby agreed as follows:-

Article I — The Viceroy and Governor-General of India may at any time after the ratification of this agreement assume the civil and military administration of so much of the *Wazarat* of Gilgit Province (herein after referred to as the "said territory") of the State of Jammu and Kashmir as lies beyond the right bank of the river Indus, but notwithstanding anything in this agreement the said territory shall continue to be included within the dominions of His Highness the Maharaja of Jammu and Kashmir.

Article II — In recognition of the fact that the said territory continues to be included within the dominion of His Highness the Maharaja of Jammu and Kashmir, salutes and customary honours shall be paid in the said territory of the administration on the occasion of the birthday of His Highness, Baisakhi, Dussehra, Basant-Panchmi and on such other occasions as may be agreed upon by His Excellency the Viceroy and Governor-General of India. The flag of His Highness will be flown at the official headquarters of the agency throughout the year.

Article III—In normal circumstances no British Indian troops shall be dispatched through that portion of the *Wazarat* of Gilgit Province which lies beyond the left bank of the river Indus.

Article IV—All rights pertaining to mining are reserved to His Highness the Maharaja of Jammu and Kashmir. The grant of prospecting licences and mining leases will be made during the period of the agreement mentioned below.

Article V—This agreement shall remain in force for sixty years from the date of its ratification and the leases will terminate at the end of that period.

Signed and exchanged at Jammu this 26th day of the month of March, 1935.

Notes

1   The word *Dard* was first used by Dr. G.W. Leitner, who cited evidence from Western classical sources and identify *Dardae* with *Darada* of Sanskrit writers.

2   Ahmad Hassan Dani, *History of Northern Areas of Pakistan*, Islamabad: National Institute of Historical and Cultural Research, 1991, pp. 161-162.

3   Hashmatullah Khan, *Tarikh-i-Jammu,* p. 679.

4   NN Raina, *Kashmir Politics and Imperialist Manoeuvres 1846 –1980.* New Delhi: Patriot Publishers 1988, p. 11.

5   Ibid., p. 29.

6   Ibid., p. 29.

7   Arthur Neve, *Thirty Years in Kashmir.*

8   As quoted by FM Hassnain, *British Policy Towards Kashmir,* (1846–1921), New Delhi: Sterling Publishers, 1974, p. 61.

9   Colonel Algernon Durand, *The Making of a Frontier,* London, 1900, p. 66.

10 Hashmathullah, no. 3, p. 449.

11 Ibid., pp. 449-450.

12 Franke, *Antiquities II,* p. 131.

13 *Akhbar-i-Ludhiana* (Ludhiana) May 2, 1840. *Delhi Urdu Akhbar* (Delhi), May 17, 1840, as cited by C.I. Dutta in *Ladakah and Western Himalayan Politics,* New Delhi, 1973, 126.

14 Alastair Lamb, *Crisis in Kashmir,* 1947-1966. London, 1966, p. 145.

15 Francis Watsan, The Frontier of China, London, 1966.

16 Sisir Gupta, *Kashmir A Study in India-Pakistan Relations,* New Delhi: Asia Publishing House, 1966, p. 428.

17 Ibid.

18 Ibid., p. 429.

19 Francis Watson, no. 15, p. 166.

3

Dawn of Independence
and the Tribal Raid

S. Kalyanaraman

Jammu & Kashmir emerged as a distinct political entity in 1846 with the assumption of sovereignty by the Dogra ruler Gulab Singh. Till then, it had successively been a part of the realms of various Hindu, Buddhist, Muslim and Sikh dynasties — each with its centre of political power in other parts of what we today refer to as South Asia. During the rule of the last of these dynasties — the Sikh — Gulab Singh was conferred a fief over Jammu for his contribution to the conquest of Kashmir. He subsequently expanded this realm by conquering Ladakh and Baltistan in the late 1830s. With the onset of the decline of Sikh power at the end of the First Anglo-Sikh War in 1846, Gulab Singh espied an opportunity to make even more substantial gains and concluded an agreement with the British colonial authorities in India. Under this Treaty of Amritsar, signed on March 16, 1846, he acknowledged the supremacy of the British Government and in return acquired sovereignty over the hill country between the rivers Indus and Ravi, including Jammu, Kashmir, Ladakh, Gilgit and Baltistan. While he had a free hand in conducting the internal affairs of this State of Jammu & Kashmir as well as to ensure his dynastic succession, Britain — the paramount power — was exclusively responsible, like in the case of all other princely states, for defence, foreign affairs and communications.[1] This state of affairs continued essentially unchanged till Britain wound up its empire in India.

Hari Singh's ascendance to the throne of Jammu & Kashmir in 1925 coincided with the awakening of mass political consciousness throughout India, which was spearheaded by a renewed and invigorated Indian National Congress under the direction of Mahatma Gandhi. This found an echo in Jammu & Kashmir as well, though the popular movement in this princely state was directed more at the absolutist rule of the Dogra dynasty. During the course of the 1930s, Sheikh Abdullah, who had returned after completing his education at Lahore and Aligarh, spearheaded this popular movement through the medium of the All Jammu & Kashmir Muslim Conference, which he had founded in October 1932 to represent the State's Muslim population. But animated as he was by progressive and secular ideals, Abdullah became increasingly dissatisfied with the sectarian approach to political struggle and began to make common cause with the Indian National Congress.

Prem Nath Bazaz has pointed out that an indication of such non-sectarian thinking was evident in the presidential address of the very first session of the Muslim Conference: "The Kashmir movement is not communal but has come into existence to get the grievances of all classes of people redressed. We assure our Hindu and Sikh brothers that we are prepared to help them in the same manner as we do the Muslamans. Our country cannot progress until we learn to live amicably with one another."

Before the decade of the 1930s closed, Abdullah steered the transformation of the All Jammu & Kashmir Muslim Conference into the All Jammu & Kashmir National Conference. According to Bazaz, only three of the 179 delegates attending the June 1939 special session of the party, at which the transformation was effected, opposed the move.[2]

In 1946, the National Conference formally joined the All-India States Peoples' Congress (AISPC), and Abdullah became its president on the eve of Indian independence.[3] It would be pertinent to note here that the AISPC was the Congress party's vehicle for integrating the States Peoples' movements with its own anti-colonial struggle, and its objective was the attainment of full responsible government by the peoples of the princely states as integral parts of free India.[4]

However, the opponents of Abdullah's move within the party teamed up with others of similar ideological persuasion to revive the All Jammu & Kashmir Muslim Conference in June 1941. This resulted in a growing political-ideological divide in the state similar to, and in effect a carry over of, the ideological struggle between the Congress and the Muslim League in British India.[5] Abdullah's subsequent gesture in requesting Jinnah to mediate between the two parties proved to be a grave mistake and merely contributed to deepening the divide. For, the Quaid-e-Azam followed up his anodyne remarks on the need for the two parties to unite "around one platform, one organisation and one banner" with the decidedly partisan statement that "99 per cent of the Moslems who met me are of the opinion that the Moslem Conference alone is the representative organ of the State Moslems." Embittered and outraged at such obvious partisanship and misrepresentation of the actual state of affairs, Abdullah resorted to violent abuse. In the judgement of Lord Birdwood, this episode foreclosed any future possibility of Abdullah and the National Conference making common cause with Jinnah and the Muslim League.[6]

The Lapse of Paramountcy and Hari Singh's Conundrum

The British decision to quit India brought forth the question of the status of the princely states on the one hand and the relationship between them and India and Pakistan on the other. London's policy in this regard was put forward by the British Cabinet Mission in 1946, which declared that Britain's paramountcy over the princely states would not be transferred to the successor government(s) but would simply lapse, meaning, rights that had been surrendered by Indian princes to the paramount power "will return to the States." At the same time, it envisaged a "Union of India embracing both British India and the States" to deal with foreign affairs, defence and communications, but guided by the caveat that the princely states "will retain all subjects and powers other than those ceded to the Union."[7] Though Indian parties rejected the Cabinet Mission's proposals, its statements on the future of the princely states became the basis for the relationship of princely states with independent India and Pakistan. The British Government acknowledged this in the partition plan of June 3, 1947 which specifically declared that the envisaged partition and transfer of power do not extend to the princely states and that its "policy towards Indian States contained in the Cabinet Mission Memorandum of May 12, 1946 remains unchanged."[8]

An arrangement of the sort that prevailed during colonial rule was indeed necessary given that the British Raj had evolved as a single economic unit with common customs, transit and communications, posts and telegraphs, etc., under a system of co-ordinated administration on all matters of common concern. This was largely a result of the Crown Representative (to the princely states) and the Viceroy (of British-ruled territories) having been one and the same person. With the severance of the British link, an alternative mechanism had to be put in place to avoid chaos, which would affect the States first and foremost. Moreover, the territories of practically all princely states, barring Jammu & Kashmir, were encompassed within, or exclusively contiguous to, the envisaged territories of India and Pakistan. Hence, as pointed out by Mountbatten in his July 1947 address to the Chamber of Princes, they would not be able to evade "certain geographical compulsions."[9] Only two among the 565 princely states — Junagadh and Hyderabad — sought to evade these geographical compulsions, though unsuccessfully.

Jammu & Kashmir was in a class of its own, given that it shared borders with both India and Pakistan as well as with Afghanistan and China. In addition, its Hindu Maharaja ruled over a population that then comprised a little over 77 per cent Muslims. Hari Singh was truly on the horns of a dilemma. Acceding to India was an attractive option given his own religious affiliation and familial antecedents. But this choice would mean the political empowerment of Abdullah and his own loss of power, status and prestige, given the Congress party's inclinations and Nehru's close friendship with Hari Singh's political nemesis, Sheikh Abdullah, who was then serving a jail sentence for launching the 'Quit Kashmir' movement against the Maharaja in 1946. The Maharaja seems to have gone to the extent of characterising the Congress party as his "enemy".[10] On the other hand, acceding to Pakistan appeared to be a better option, given the assurances provided by Muslim League leaders about respecting his internal sovereignty. The Maharaja had also received pledges of continued loyalty, though conditional upon his opting for Pakistan, from the leaders of the Muslim Conference and, telegraphically, from the chieftains of Chitral, Hunza and other small outlying territories of the state. But some of these pledges soon turned into threats of military invasion, as happened in the case of the Mehtar of Chitral and the Nawab of Dir.[11] Hari Singh reckoned that, given the extreme emotions evoked by communal polarisation, his accession to Pakistan would not stop future attempts to divest him of his rule over a Muslim-majority population.

At the same time, he had also been witnessing the horrors that began to accompany the Muslim League's demand for a separate State, beginning with the call for Direct Action in August 1946. Communal riots began to break out across northern India, including rather explosively in neighbouring Punjab. The subsequent partition of Punjab unleashed a further orgy of violence and the mass exodus of people. Some 200,000 Hindu, Muslim and Sikh refugees passed through Jammu *en route* to their respective 'homelands'. An earlier batch of Hindu and Sikh refugees had also flowed into the State from the North West Frontier Province in the run-up to and aftermath of the referendum held there to decide its political future. Lord Birdwood has pointed out that it would be a fair assessment to say that Hari Singh's hesitation about acceding to Pakistan can be attributed to the desire to save his State and especially his Dogra subjects — on whose support his dynasty's rule had rested for four generations — from such terrible slaughter. In addition, he had genuine reasons of state to ensure that such a situation did not come to pass. Muslims comprised over thirty-five per cent of the military forces of this 'Hindu Dogra' kingdom, and fifty per cent of the police force in Jammu province alone. The civil administration was also staffed by a mix of Hindus, Sikhs and Muslims. Any communal disturbance would bring the government machinery to a grinding halt and ultimately render his position and rule defenceless and untenable.[12]

Under the circumstances, remaining independent was an attractive option and there is speculation that Hari Singh and his Prime Minister (till mid-August 1947) Ram Chandra Kak may have toyed with such an idea. But there was practically no one else — among the leaders of the Congress and the Muslim League as well as among the Viceroy's staff and British officers serving in the Kashmir administration — who looked upon this choice favourably. Congress leaders had it conveyed through Mountbatten that Hari Singh should not make a declaration of independence, though they did not wish to exert any pressure on the Maharaja to opt for India. In addition, Mountbatten also informed the Maharaja that he has been assured by Indian leaders that they would not regard Kashmir's accession to Pakistan as an unfriendly act and would not raise any objection in this regard.[13]

In the case of the Muslim League, the fact that Pakistan's "very name and concept ... included Kashmir as an integral part" meant that its leaders did not conceive of an independent Kashmir. According to Chaudhri Muhammad Ali, Prime Minister of Pakistan between 1955 and 1956, Jinnah used to tell his fellow Muslim League leaders and followers that Kashmir "will fall into our lap like a ripe fruit" because he was convinced "that a dispassionate consideration of the relevant facts of population and geography, the economic and cultural ties, and even the Maharaja's dynastic interest would inevitably point toward accession with Pakistan."[14]

The Labour Government, which was then in power in Britain, also did not view with favour the independence option for princely states, though most Conservatives did. Speaking in the House of Commons, Clement Attlee expressed the hope in July 1947 that all princely states "will, in due course, find their appropriate place within one or the other of the new Dominions." The British Prime Minister added that if any ruler were to assert independence, then his advice to the latter would be: "Take your time and think again. I hope that no irrevocable decision will be taken prematurely." Lord Listowel, the Secretary of State for India, informed the House of Lords in July 1947 that the British government "do not, of course, propose to recognise any States as separate international entities."[15]

In India, Mountbatten gave similar advice to the princely states. Speaking to the Chamber of Princes on July 25, 1947, he cautioned them against trying to evade geographical compulsions and pointed out: "You cannot run away from the Dominion Government which is your neighbour any more than you can run away from the subjects for whose welfare you are responsible."[16] With specific regard to Jammu & Kashmir, Mountbatten visited the state in June 1947 and urged Hari Singh and his Prime Minister Ram Chandra Kak not to make a declaration of independence (to which they agreed) and to take measures to ascertain the will of the people on which Dominion to accede to. He pointed out that the state would otherwise find itself in a dangerous situation without "the support of one of the two Dominions." And upon his instruction, the British Resident in the State, Colonel W. F.

Webb, continued to provide them the same advice.[17] Maj.
Gen. H. L. Scott, the commander of the State Forces,
reinforced the last aspect of Mountbatten's message by
repeatedly advising the Maharaja that the army was simply
not up to the task of backing up and sustaining the
administration.[18]

Faced with a Hobson's choice, the Maharaja dithered. In
an attempt to temporarily maintain the *status quo*, he sought
'Standstill Agreements' with both Dominions, for which purpose
he sent identical telegrams to the two governments on August
12, 1947. Pakistan telegraphically conveyed its consent to this
arrangement on August 15, which provided for the continuation
of administrative arrangements for communications, supplies,
posts and telegraphs. India, for its part, telegraphed back an
invitation for the Maharaja or one of his duly authorised
ministers to fly to Delhi for the purpose of negotiating a standstill
agreement.[19] The Government of India's stated policy in regard
to standstill agreements was: 'no standstill agreement
without accession'. It had been framed, and announced on
August 1, 1947, to specifically deal with the 'no to accession'
lobby among the princely states. After independence, the
Government of India made just one exception to this policy
while dealing with the Nizam of Hyderabad. But it needs to
be pointed out that a standstill agreement in this case was
signed as late as November 29, 1947 after some rather
protracted negotiations.[20] Be that as it may, though no standstill
agreement was concluded between India and Jammu &
Kashmir, New Delhi continued to give effect to the existing
arrangements in practice.

India and the Princely State of Jammu & Kashmir

While they waited for the Maharaja to make up his mind,
Indian and Pakistani leaders adopted completely contrasting
approaches towards Jammu & Kashmir. Indian leaders were
in an especially delicate situation when it came to dealing
with the State. On the one hand, they wanted Hari Singh to

accede to India, but on the other they were insistent upon the Maharaja firstly releasing Sheikh Abdullah — "the popular leader of the people" as a Congress Working Committee resolution on Kashmir described him — from prison and then arriving at a *modus vivendi* with his National Conference. All the principal leaders of the Congress party were convinced that Hari Singh had no choice but to bring Abdullah into the governance structure before taking a decision on accession.

It was Mahatma Gandhi who first broached this issue with the Maharaja during his first visit to the State in early August 1947. In a report sent to Nehru and Patel, Gandhi noted the Maharaja and Maharani's admission that "with the lapse of British Paramountcy the true Paramountcy of the people of Kashmir would commence. (And) However much they might wish to join the Union (of India), they would have to make the choice in accordance with the wishes of the people." However, his discussions with the royals did not include the modalities of ascertaining the popular wish. Gandhi then summarised the view expressed to him by Bakshi Ghulam Mohammad that the result of a free popular vote either on the basis of "adult franchise or on the existing register would be in favour of Kashmir joining the Union" provided Abdullah and the other imprisoned leaders of the National Conference were released, all the bans were revoked and Ram Chandra Kak was removed from the prime ministership. Some writers have read too much into this reference to Kak and go to the extent of stating that his subsequent dismissal occurred because of the pressure exerted by the Mahatma.[21] But Gandhi was merely conveying the views expressed to him by Bakshi, and he noted *sotto voce* that the latter was probably echoing "the general sentiment". For, the Mahatma seems to have heard much about Kak's unpopularity from the people and even conveyed this to the prime minister during their two interviews.[22]

Patel's correspondence sheds particular light on how independent India dealt with Jammu & Kashmir. Writing to

Hari Singh on July 3, 1947, Patel assured him that contrary to his "considerable misapprehension" neither the Congress nor Nehru personally were his enemies. Drawing attention to the "difficult and delicate situation" in which Jammu & Kashmir was placed at that point in time, he stressed that the State's interest lay in joining the Indian Union without delay. On the same day, in a separate letter, Patel advised the State's Prime Minister to reconsider the issue of releasing Abdullah from detention "purely in the interest of Kashmir State." Even on the very eve of the tribal raid, Patel urged the State's new Prime Minister, Mahajan, to make "a substantial gesture to win Abdullah's support" so as to be able to "crush the disruptive forces which are being raised and organised" by Pakistan.[23]

Nehru too seems to have been generally aware that there were preparations afoot in Pakistan's Punjab and North West Frontier Province "to enter Kashmir in considerable numbers [and] to take some big action" after the onset of winter physically cut the State off from India. He was of the firm view that Pakistan's designs could be countered only if the National Conference sided with the Maharaja. It was, therefore, imperative that Hari Singh extended a hand of friendship to Abdullah so that "there might be this popular support against Pakistan". Writing to Patel in this regard in late September 1947, Nehru appeared convinced that the Maharaja had no choice but to release Abdullah and other National Conference leaders, make a friendly approach towards them, seek their co-operation and then "declare adhesion to the Indian Union". But the important thing, he noted, was that this had to happen without delay before the onset of winter isolated the State from the rest of India.[24]

The task at hand was a rather delicate one, given that Indian leaders had to balance between the imperatives of supporting the Maharaja's government while at the same time convincing him of the need to politically accommodate Sheikh Abdullah and the National Conference. Patel, who was principally responsible for dealing with the Princely States, sought to gently coax and cajole the Maharaja and his principal ministers into adopting a more favourable view of the Indian Dominion. He did not limit himself to exhortations about the imperative of arriving at an early accommodation with Abdullah and the National Conference, but also expedited the provision of practical help as and when these were sought especially after violence broke out in Poonch and the State authorities began to accuse Pakistan of providing assistance to "evilly-disposed persons."[25]

The letters Patel exchanged with the authorities in Srinagar clearly demonstrate how he handled this affair. In the third week of September 1947, he wrote to the Maharaja that there is full realisation in India about his difficult situation and assured him that New Delhi will do its best to help the State. Ten days later, he again wrote to Hari Singh expressing his pleasure at the general amnesty that the Maharaja had proclaimed and assured him that work on the establishment/ improvement of telegraph, telephone, wireless and road communications between the State and India is being expedited. Earlier he had recommended to the Indian Minister for Refugee Relief and Rehabilitation that the disrupted air communications between India and the State should be promptly restored.[26] But on the crucial issue of supplying military equipment to Jammu & Kashmir, his efforts were thwarted by British military officers who were then at the helm of the Indian armed forces and by Auchinleck's Supreme Headquarters.[27] India's assistance to the State during this period also extended to the personnel front. Patel recommended to Defence Minister Baldev Singh that the services of Lt. Col. Kashmir Singh Katoch of the Indian Army be loaned to Jammu & Kashmir to serve as commander of the State Forces after the retirement of Scott at the end of September 1947. He, of course, did not overlook the advantages of this arrangement for India, pointing out to Baldev Singh "the overriding consideration of having our own man as Commander-in-Chief of the Kashmir State Forces."[28] Mehr Chand Mahajan, then serving as a Justice of the East Punjab High Court, was similarly loaned to the Maharaja to serve as his Prime Minister.[29]

What the Indian leadership thereby sought was to strengthen the Maharaja's hands by providing him aid to deal effectively with the challenges confronting him within the State. At the same time, they also sought to impress upon him what was clearly evident to them—that politically accommodating Abdullah and the National Conference within the State's governance structure would similarly strengthen his hands in dealing with these threats. Further, given that there was sufficient evidence that the violence in Poonch was receiving encouragement and assistance from across the other border with Pakistan, coupled with Abdullah's own favourable inclinations towards India and the Congress leadership, Hari Singh could boldly take the next logical step of acceding to the Indian Dominion.

Pakistan's 'Tribal Raid'

Pakistan's actions were in direct contrast to the delicate balancing that India sought to perform. Pakistani leaders were utterly convinced that Jammu & Kashmir had to accede to their Dominion. Initially, in the wake of the 3rd June announcement, Jinnah wished to visit Jammu & Kashmir in order to explain to the Maharaja in person what an association between Pakistan and his State "might mean in theory and in practice." But Mountbatten dissuaded him from undertaking such a visit, just like he headed Nehru off from visiting the State.[30] Jinnah repeatedly expressed the wish to visit the State after the official establishment of Pakistan as well. According to Mahajan, the Quaid-e-Azam cited 'health reasons' for such a visit, adding that he would come as a private citizen. But Chaudhri Muhammad Ali, who was then Secretary-General of the Pakistan Government as well as Cabinet Secretary, has recorded that Jinnah actually wanted to visit Kashmir in the middle of September "to have a friendly talk with the Maharaja". Whatever were Jinnah's actual motives, Hari Singh suspected the worst and politely refused, citing the tense circumstances then prevailing and his consequent inability to accord to the Quaid-e-Azam the honours and security arrangements due to the head of state of an important neighbour.[31] However, even as Jinnah was expressing his wish to visit the State in mid-September, actions were afoot to militarily overthrow the Maharaja's government and engineer the State's accession to Pakistan. For, an opportunity had presented itself in the form of popular disaffection in Poonch province.

Poonch was a very poor region and military service was one of the principal outlets for employment to its residents. During the Second World War, some 70,000 out of a total population of 400,000 served in the British Indian Army. At the end of the war, some 60,000 of these soldiers were rapidly demobilised. Upon their return home, they discovered that several new taxes had been imposed resulting in economic hardship.[32] Sardar Ibrahim Khan, a young lawyer who belonged to the Sudhan tribe in Poonch and who was also a member of the State's Muslim Conference, slipped into Pakistan sometime in August 1947. And, during the course of the next few weeks, he established contacts with Pakistani leaders, including Prime Minister Liaquat Ali Khan, in order to obtain military assistance for initiating an armed struggle of liberation.[33]

Even as Ibrahim Khan was doing the rounds in Pakistan, a party of about thirty Pakistani nationals infiltrated into Poonch at the end of August and began to incite the Sutti and Sudhan tribes in the province to agitate against the Maharaja and in favour of accession to Pakistan. Maj. Gen. Scott, the Commander of the State Forces, recorded that the actual result of such incitement was a march undertaken in early September by about 10,000 local residents to Poonch town to air their local grievances, principally high food prices, though they also raised slogans demanding accession to Pakistan. On September 9, 1947, they were dispersed by the State troops at the town of Bagh. Twenty demonstrators died in this clash. Sardar Abdul Qayyum Khan, who was a principal organiser of the demonstration, and three of his compatriots fled to the mountains and began organising resistance to the State troops.[34] Scott has recorded that there was no further trouble in the province till the end of his tenure on September 29, 1947.[35]

In the meantime, Ibrahim Khan's plea for help led to two key meetings in Lahore on September 12. The first was at the office of Sardar Shaukat Hayat Khan, a Minister in the Punjab provincial government; and the second, that evening, at the residence of Pakistan's Prime Minister Liaquat Ali Khan. The aim of these meetings was to chart out a course of military action in Jammu & Kashmir in order to use the words of a prominent Muslim League leader Mian Iftikharuddin — "prevent the State's accession to India." What he left unsaid was that this was to be achieved by overthrowing the Maharaja's government and engineering the State's forcible accession to Pakistan.

Two different plans were discussed at the meeting. Akbar Khan, who was then Director of Weapons and Equipment at General Headquarters in Rawalpindi, had prepared one, titled *Armed Revolt in Kashmir*, at the express request of Iftikharuddin. Given that "open interference or aggression by Pakistan was obviously undesirable," Akbar Khan proposed that Kashmiris be strengthened internally while at the same time directing efforts to block the routes through which India could technically provide military assistance to the Jammu & Kashmir government. But his plan was not approved and he was assigned the limited task of clandestinely diverting 4,000 military rifles meant for the police as well as stocks of old ammunition for the action in Kashmir. He has recorded that at General Headquarters in Rawalpindi he received help from some Army and Air Force officers as well as the Commissioner of the district in collecting weapons, ammunition, winter clothing, rations, funds and volunteers for Kashmir. He also notes that Pakistan's Prime Minister arranged for the procurement of 250 light machine guns from a war dump in Italy to be utilised for the military action in Kashmir, though what eventually arrived were Sten guns.

The September 12 meetings chose the second plan presented that day.[36] Shaukat Hayat Khan had conceived this plan, which involved the employment of two different groups of officers and other ranks of the erstwhile Indian National Army (INA) under his overall command. One group was to operate across the Punjab border under Zaman Kiani who was a former INA officer. The other was to function north of Rawalpindi under the leadership of Khurshid Anwar, a former British Indian Army officer. Anwar was a Pakistani citizen from the Punjab and, despite Hayat Khan's lack of confidence in him, he was especially chosen by "the authorities concerned" because of his earlier role in raising the Muslim League's National Guard and more importantly for delivering the North West Frontier Province to Pakistan by rousing communal passions among people who had for long remained under the sway of the Frontier Gandhi and his Khudai Khidmatgars.[37]

Even as this plan was being set in motion, an unofficial economic blockade was imposed on Jammu & Kashmir. Maj. Gen. Scott, whose tenure ended on September 29, reported that "Whatever may be the policy of the Pakistan government, Rawalpindi is turning on the heat. No sugar or petrol are reaching Kashmir." And he categorically dismissed the claim made by Pakistani leaders that this was a result of Muslim drivers refusing to carry goods because they were being attacked by Sikhs *en route*. The government in Srinagar listed rice, wheat, cloth, salt and petrol as items being withheld by Pakistani authorities. Abdul Haq, the District Commissioner of Rawalpindi, and his brother Ikramul Haq, a civilian official of the Pakistan Ministry of Defence, played a crucial role in this regard, a fact the then British High Commissioner to Pakistan admitted at that time. It is indeed food for thought that an official of the Ministry of Defence was involved in issues that were economic in nature. Evidence, *albeit* circumstantial, that the Haq brothers' action was an integral part of a larger Pakistani game plan has come from an account given by the then Commander-in-Chief of the Pakistan Army, General Frank Messervy. Shortly before the October 21/22 tribal invasion, George Cunningham, the Governor of the North West Frontier Province (NWFP), informed Messervy that the Chief Minister of the province was encouraging and organising tribesmen for an invasion of Jammu & Kashmir and asked the Commander-in-Chief what the official policy of the federal government in Karachi was. Messervy's emphatic advice to Liaquat Ali Khan that such a course of action should be avoided, led within a few days to a conference in Lahore between Jinnah, Liaquat and the Chief Minister of NWFP. The outcome of this conference can be gauged from events that subsequently unfolded the tribal invasion of Jammu & Kashmir. Shaukat Hayat Khan, under whose overall command the plan was implemented, confirmed in a 1997 BBC television programme that Jinnah himself had provided approval for the invasion.[38] Messervy also obtained circumstantial evidence with regard to the role of the Haq brothers. Upon hearing rumours that the invasion of Jammu & Kashmir was being planned at the District Commissioner's residence in Rawalpindi, Messervy used a pretext to despatch one of his officers thither, who found Abdul Haq presiding over a meeting of tribal leaders involved in the invasion.[39]

As mentioned earlier, Khurshid Anwar was responsible for operations north of Rawalpindi along Jammu & Kashmir's border with the North West Frontier Province. After being assigned this task at the September 12 meeting in Lahore, he established contact with tribal leaders in the NWFP to recruit fighters and reinforce the forces under his command. He knew them well from the time he had earlier mobilised them to cast their lot with Pakistan. One advantage of employing Pathan fighters lay in their deep involvement in the transport business, which meant easy access to buses and lorries in which the fighters can move swiftly towards their target. Willing fighters were especially aplenty in the Province and all were itching for *jihad*. Alastair Lamb notes that the decision to actually recruit tribesmen for an invasion of Jammu & Kashmir was probably taken in the second week of October. For, the plan that had been conceived earlier at the September 12 conference in Lahore faced two main problems. The first was the lack of adequate motor transport, and the second was obtaining access to the Jhelum Valley Road, which was dominated by a number of bridges guarded, *albeit*, by small numbers of State troops. The employment of tribesmen held out the promise of solving both these problems. The tribesmen would provide motor transport, and at the same time help to terrorise and overwhelm the State troops. In addition, contacts were also established with the Muslim elements of the 4th Jammu & Kashmir Rifles, which was guarding the frontier bridges.

The tribal invasion began on the night of October 21/22, 1947, after the Muslim elements of the 4th J&K Rifles disposed off their sleeping Dogra colleagues and joined the tribesmen under Anwar's command. Muzaffarabad was quickly taken. Uri too fell soon though after some spirited defence by the remainder of the State troops. Baramula fell on the fourth day of the invasion. Though the road to Srinagar was open, the tribesmen gave in to their urge for rapine and massacre, and resumed their advance only after another two days.[40]

Accession to India

Pakistan's 'tribal' invasion of Jammu & Kashmir left the Maharaja with no choice but to seek Indian help. The first formal news of the invasion reached New Delhi on the evening of October 24, with the arrival of the State's Deputy Prime Minister Ram Lal Batra. Batra carried a letter of accession to India from Hari Singh as well as separate personal letters for Nehru and Patel from the Maharaja.[41]

A meeting of the Defence Committee of the Cabinet (DCC) was promptly convened for the very next morning to discuss the grave situation that had arisen in Jammu & Kashmir. After due deliberation, V. P. Menon, Sam Manekshaw and Wing Commander Dewan were despatched to the State to make an assessment of the prevailing political and military situation there. At the same time, the Indian military was tasked to fly in arms and ammunition to Srinagar as well as to prepare contingency plans for the provision of direct military assistance to the State authorities. The deliberations that eventually led to the above decisions throw much light on the thinking of Indian leaders at this point in time. Nehru firmly stated that the Maharaja's government could save the situation only by completely co-operating with, and bringing into the government, the popular forces represented by Abdullah and the National Conference. Mountbatten then raised the issue of the State's accession to India.[42]

It would be necessary to note here that after the Junagadh crisis broke out, Nehru had proposed at the very first meeting of the Defence Committee on September 30, 1947 that disputes over territory "should be decided by a referendum or plebiscite of the people concerned" and that it is the Indian government's desire that decisions in this regard "should be made in accordance with the wishes of the people concerned." Nehru mentioned this again on the same day in the course of a meeting of the Joint Defence Council attended by Liaquat Ali Khan. But Pakistani leaders kept insisting on the ruler's prerogative in this regard.[43] Of course, after Maharaja Hari Singh acceded to India in the face of the tribal raid unleashed by Pakistan on Jammu & Kashmir, they changed their tune and began to parrot the argument about ascertaining the wishes of the people.

Consequently, when Mountbatten raised the issue of Jammu & Kashmir's accession to India at the eighth meeting of the DCC on October 25, 1947, he pointed out that the Maharaja would find it difficult to accept the advice that he should ascertain the wishes of his people under the grave circumstances then prevailing. Mountbatten suggested that one solution could be for the State to temporarily accede to India, and after the tribal raiders had been expelled and law and order had been restored, the people's wishes with regard to accession could be ascertained. V. P. Menon seconded this suggestion, stating that the great advantage of immediate accession would be that it would enable India to promptly despatch armed assistance to the State. But Nehru, Patel and some other members of the Committee expressed doubts about the advisability of Jammu & Kashmir acceding to India at that point in time. Both Patel and Nehru voiced the view that there could be no legal objection to the provision of armed assistance at the express request of a State. Nehru also pointed out that the Indian position at that juncture was rather tricky, given that, accepting the State's accession "would be considered a manoeuvre," while on the other hand Pakistan would readily raise objections to India sending armed assistance whether or not accession was accepted. His own view was that accepting accession "might lead to greater difficulties".

However, after receiving Menon's and Manekshaw's appreciations of the situation prevailing in the State the next day, that the tribal raiders were advancing rapidly and were just 35 miles from Srinagar, the Defence Committee decided to accept Jammu & Kashmir's accession. It also decided that an interim government under Sheikh Abdullah should be set up simultaneously.[44] While accepting the Maharaja's letter of accession, Mountbatten wrote to Hari Singh that in accordance with the Indian government's policy a reference would be made to the people on this issue after "law and order have been restored in Kashmir and its soil cleared of the invader."[45]

Indian troops were flown into Srinagar on the morning of October 27, and began to drive the raiders back, reoccupying Uri on November 14. With the tribesmen now pushed back to their point of entry into Kashmir, their subsequent operations naturally extended to the south and south east of Muzaffarabad.

With the onset of winter, a line running through Mirpur, Kotli and Poonch became stabilised. In the spring of 1948, the tribal lashkars were backstopped by the deployment in Jammu & Kashmir territory of Pakistani troops. Though Indian troops did make progress through 1948, they could not completely drive out the raiders and the Pakistani army, thus perpetuating the division of the Dogra kingdom into the Indian State of Jammu & Kashmir and Pakistan-occupied Kashmir.

Conclusion

When Britain decided to wind up the Raj, Maharaja Hari Singh found himself between a rock and a hard place. Acceding to India was a guaranteed recipe for loss of power, prestige and status. And in the communally polarised and violence-marred atmosphere of 1947, acceding to Pakistan also appeared to guarantee the eventual loss of power to rule over his Muslim citizens. He, therefore, naturally dithered. Indian leaders sought to coax him into accommodating Sheikh Abdullah and the National Conference within the State's governance structure before taking a decision on accession. At the same time, they tried to mollify him by providing assistance to shore up his government's ability to deal with the internal security situation in the State. In contrast, Pakistani leaders decided to employ coercive economic pressure and naked military aggression to overthrow the Maharaja and force the State's accession to their Dominion. For this purpose, they exploited local disaffection in Poonch to launch a full-scale tribal invasion of the State designed to 'liberate' its Muslim citizens from the rule of their Hindu Maharaja. Faced with this onslaught from Pakistan, Hari Singh was forced to seek Indian assistance.

The Maharaja's call for assistance to tackle the Pakistan-organised tribal invasion placed Indian leaders on the horns of a dilemma. For, India's provision of military assistance to Jammu & Kashmir would lead to objections by Pakistan. And in the worst case, Karachi could even claim a right to send its own troops into the State, which was tellingly demonstrated by Jinnah's unsuccessful attempt on October 27, 1947 to launch Pakistani troops into Jammu & Kashmir. On the other hand, an Indian decision to accept the State's accession as a prelude to the provision of military aid would be interpreted as a 'manoeuvre'. But given the need to promptly save the State from the depredations of the marauding tribal raiders, Indian leaders decided to accept the Maharaja's accession. Simultaneously, they convinced the Maharaja to involve the National Conference — the principal representative of the people of the State — in the State's governance structure.

A significant aspect of this Indian decision was the understanding that the people's wishes have to be taken into account on this issue. While accepting Jammu & Kashmir's accession, Mountbatten wrote to the Maharaja that the Indian government's acceptance of accession was subject to a reference to ascertain the wishes of the people after the State's soil has been cleared of the invaders and, law and order have been restored. Though Nehru too gave such an undertaking, Pakistan's decision to emplace its own troops in Jammu & Kashmir territory in the spring of 1948 and its refusal to consider withdrawing them despite UN calls to do so, rendered the Indian undertaking impossible to implement. In subsequent decades, India consequently had to make do with other arrangements. Free elections on the basis of universal suffrage were held in September-October 1951 to elect a Constituent Assembly, which subsequently ratified (on November 20, 1951) the Maharaja's decision to accede to India.

Notes

[1] V. P. Menon, *Integration of the Indian States* Chennai: Orient Longman, 1997 pp. 390-91; Josef Korbel, *Danger in Kashmir,* Princeton: Princeton University Press, 1966, pp. 12-14.

2   Prem Nath Bazaz, *Kashmir in Crucible,* New Delhi: Pamposh Publications, 1967, pp. 34-35.

3   C. Dasgupta, *War and Diplomacy in Kashmir 1947-48,* New Delhi: Sage Publications 2002, p. 35.

4   Sisir Gupta, *Kashmir: A Study in India-Pakistan Relations,* Bombay: Asia Publishers, 1966, p. 37.

5   Matin Zuberi, "The Problem of Kashmir," in Guy Wint, ed., *Asia Handbook,* Harmondsworth, Middlesex: Penguin Books, 1969, p. 505.

6   Cited in Lord Birdwood, *Two Nations and Kashmir,* Srinagar: Gulshan Books, 2005, p. 62.

7   The texts of the Cabinet Mission's "Memorandum on States' Treaties and Paramountcy" and of the Cabinet Mission Statement are reprinted in *Constitutional Relations Between Britain and India, The Transfer of Power 1942-7. Vol. VII: The Cabinet Mission 23 March – 29 June 1946,* edited by Nicholas Mansergh, London: Her Majesty's Stationery Office, 1978, Documents 262 and 303.

8   The text of the 3rd June Plan can be found in *Constitutional Relations Between Britain and India, The Transfer of Power 1942-7. Vol. XI: The Mountbatten Viceroyalty: Announcement and Reception of the 3rd June Plan 31st May – 7th July 1947,* edited by Penderel Moon, London: Her Majesty's Stationery Office, 1982, Document 45.

9   The full text of Mountbatten's 25th July 1947 "Address To A Special Full Meeting of the Chamber of Princes" can be found as Appendix X in *Mountbatten's Report on the Last Viceroyalty: 22nd March – 15th August 1947,* edited by Lionel Carter, New Delhi: Manohar, 2003, pp. 381-85.

10 Hari Singh seems to have said so in a conversation with Rai Bahadur Gopal Das, who conveyed it to Sardar Patel prompting the latter to write to the Maharaja assuring him that this is not true. Vallabhbhai Patel to Hari Singh, 3rd July 1947, in *Sardar Patel's Correspondence 1945-1950: Vol. 1 – New Light on Kashmir,* edited by Durga Das, Ahmedabad: Navjivan Publishing House, 1970, p. 33.

[11] Mehr Chand Mahajan, *Looking Back;* New Delhi: Asia Publishing House, 1963, p. 130; Prem Shankar Jha, *The Origins of a Dispute: Kashmir 1947,* New Delhi: Oxford University Press, 2003, pp. 55-56.

[12] The above analysis has been drawn from: Prem Shankar Jha, *The Origins of a Dispute:* pp. 46, 54-58; Lord Birdwood, *Two Nations and Kashmir,* pp. 53-54; Mehr Chand Mahajan, *Looking Back,* pp. 130, 144; H. V. Hodson, *The Great Divide: Britain – India – Pakistan,* Karachi: Oxford University Press, 1985 edn., 1993 reprint, p. 445.

[13] *Mountbatten's Report on the Last Viceroyalty,* p. 194; Mountbatten's June 1948 speech to the East Indian Association in London is cited in Matin Zuberi, "no 5," p. 506.

[14] Chaudhri Muhammad Ali, *The Emergence of Pakistan,* New York: Columbia University Press, 1967, pp. 283, 287, 297.

[15] Cited in Sisir Gupta, no 4, pp. 76, 77.

[16] Mountbatten's 25th July 1947 "Address to a Special Full Meeting of the chamber of Princes," reprinted as Appendix in *Mountbatten's Report on the Last Viceroyalty,* pp. 381-85.

[17] *Ibid.,* p. 195.

[18] Lord Birdwood, no 6, p. 55. Prem Shankar Jha has brought out that Scott was personally inclined towards, and advocated, the State's accession to Pakistan. See his *The Origins of a Dispute: Kashmir 1947,* p. 18.

[19] Krishna Menon read out this telegram during his two-day, 8-hour, marathon speech at the UN. Speech on Kashmir at the United Nations Security Council's 762nd Meeting, 23rd January 1957. See *Krishna Menon on Kashmir: Speeches at United Nations,* edited by E. S. Reddy and A. K. Damodaran New Delhi: Sanchar Publishing House, 1992, p. 13.

[20] V. P. Menon, no 1, pp. 114, 317-36.

[21] See, for example, Chaudhri Muhammad Ali, no 14, p. 288.

22   Pyarelal, *Mahatma Gandhi: The Last Phase, Vol. II*, Ahmedabad: Navajivan Publishing House, 1958, pp. 357-58.

23   The 25th September 1947 CWC resolution on Kashmir was enclosed by Patel in one of his letters to the then Prime Minister of Kashmir, and has been reprinted in *Sardar Patel's Correspondence*, Document 24. The other documents referred to in the above passage are Documents 33, 34, 65.

24   *Ibid.*, Document 49.

25   The phrase is from a statement on the unrest in Poonch issued under the Maharaja's name on 12th September 1947. Cited in Josef Korbel, *Danger in Kashmir*, p. 67.

26   *Sardar Patel's Correspondence*, Documents 43, 47, 42.

27   This emerges clearly in the Minutes of the Eighth Meeting of the Indian Defence Committee of the Cabinet held on 25th October 1947. The minutes are reprinted as Appendix in Prem Shankar Jha, no 12, pp. 197-205; the reference to the issue at hand can be found on page 199.

28   *Sardar Patel's Correspondence*, Document 39.

29   On how Patel expedited this, see Mehr Chand Mahajan, no 11, p. 127.

30   Alastair Lamb, *Incomplete Partition: The Genesis of the Kashmir Dispute 1947-1948*, Oxford: Oxford University Press, 2000, p. 109; Mountbatten, however, made an allowance for the Mahatma to visit the State after the latter gave an undertaking not to make "propaganda speeches". See *Mountbatten's Report on the Last Viceroyalty*, p. 195.

31   Mehr Chand Mahajan, no 11, p. 131; Chaudhri Muhammad Ali, no 14, p. 290.

32   There are contrasting views on the new taxes. Richard Symonds, a refugee worker who travelled to Poonch via Rawalpindi in November 1947 with Nehru's express permission, was informed by the rebels that "some" of these taxes "applied to Muslims only." But Prem Shankar Jha has pointed out that there is no mention of Muslims-specific

taxes either in Webb's or Scott's reports as well as no contemporary references to them. Jha offers an alternate plausible explanation for what can only be characterised as misrepresentation of information by the rebels. See Richard Symonds, *In the Margins of Independence: A Relief Worker in India and Pakistan, 1942-1949,* Oxford: Oxford University Press, 2001, pp. 74-79; Prem Shankar Jha, no 12, p. 19.

33 Josef Korbel, no 1, p. 67; Alastair Lamb, no 30, p. 124; Akbar Khan, *Raiders in Kashmir,* Delhi: Army Publishers: p. 11.

34 C. Dasgupta, no 3, pp. 39-40; Prem Shankar Jha, no 12, pp. 18-20; Richard Symonds, no 32, p. 79.

35 The Jammu & Kashmir government issued a statement on 12th September 1947, which assured the people that normalcy has been restored as of 10th September and that efforts were on "to restore control to civil administration of the area." Cited in Josef Korbel, *Danger in Kashmir,* p. 67.

36 This narrative is drawn from Akbar Khan, no 33, pp. 10-20. Akbar Khan does not give dates in his book. The date mentioned here is drawn from Alastair Lamb, no 30, p. 125. Lamb, however, draws the rather limited conclusion that this meeting only served to shape the contacts that subsequently evolved between certain influential official and unofficial Pakistanis and the Poonch rebels.

37 Prem Shankar Jha, no 12, p. 31.

38 Cited by C. Dasgupta, no 3, p. 39.

39 Prem Shankar Jha, no 12, p. 111; Sisir Gupta, no 4, p. 104; Hodson, no 12, p. 447.

40 Alastair Lamb, no 30, pp. 132-35, 141.

41 Mehr Chand Mahajan, no 11, p. 150.

42 Minutes of the Eighth Meeting of the Defence Committee of the Cabinet, held on October 25, 1947. Reprinted as Apendix IV in Prem Shankar Jha, no 12, pp. 197-205.

[43] Cited in Hodson, no 12, pp. 435-36; C. Dasgupta, *War and Diplomacy in Kashmir*, p. 29.

[44] Minutes of the Eighth and Ninth Meetings of the Defence Committee of the Cabinet held on 25th and 26th October 1947. Reprinted as Appendices IV and V in Prem Shankar Jha, no 12, pp. 197-213.

[45] Mountbatten's letter in this regard to Hari Singh is reprinted as Appendix in Lord Birdwood, no 6, pp. 323-24.

4

Annexation of Gilgit-Baltistan: Tumultuous Events of 1947-48

Alok Bansal

Of the various myths that have been perpetuated about the events of 1947-48, none is farther from the truth than the assumption that Gilgit and Baltistan were liberated from the tyrannical rule of the Maharaja, by an indigenous movement that was led by local population. Another myth that has been propagated is that the region which has been termed as 'Northern Areas' by Pakistan was historically a separate political entity and had never been a part of the Jammu and Kashmir State but was handed over to Maharaja Hari Singh by the British on the eve of Independence. The fact is that the region that constitutes today the political entity called as 'Northern Areas' of Pakistan has never in its history existed as a composite political entity. It is, therefore, vital to understand the status of the region prior to 1947 and then analyse the events of 1947-48 to arrive at a correct appreciation of the developments in the region.

Historically, Gilgit-Baltistan evolved as two separate political entities, Dardistan or Gilgit and Baltistan. Though there were times when they were part of the same political entity,[1] the two were eventually united during the Sikh rule and even then Gilgit was captured by "Syed Nathe Shah, the commander of Sheikh Ghulam Mohi-ud-din, the Governor of Sikhs in Kashmir" in 1842,[2] where as Baltistan had been reduced to 'vassalage' in 1840 by General Zorawar Singh[3] for the Dogras, who were till then under the suzerainty of the Sikhs. The region remained a part of the common political entity during the subsequent Dogra rule. After the signing of Treaty of Amritsar in 1846, the British encouraged Gulab Singh to spread his political influence in Gilgit-Baltistan so as to establish a safe buffer state between Russia and British India. By 1870, the entire region had come under the control of the Dogras and the treaties were signed with the rulers of Hunza and Nagar making them vassals of Kashmir[4].

However, after the Russian interest in the region had become quite clear, the British forced the Maharaja to lease Gilgit and the surrounding region on and beyond the right bank of River Indus to them for 60 years in 1935.[5] Though a modicum of Maharaja's authority was maintained by way of flying his flag at the official headquarters of the agency and by way of appointment of certain state officials in Gilgit, the only real authority with the Maharaja was to grant mining licences and leases.[6] Many Pakistani scholars cite this treaty to suggest that Gilgit-Baltistan or the 'Northern Areas' were actually not a part of Kashmir State and should not be considered part of Jammu and Kashmir as far as any future settlement is concerned. However, they tend to overlook the fact that all the area south of the River Indus in Dardistan and the entire Baltistan remained under the direct control of the Maharaja and as such only a part of this present-day artificial entity called 'Northern Areas' was leased to the British. Moreover, even there the authority of Maharaja and his sovereignty was acknowledged unquestionably. He also continued to exercise suzerainty over local rulers.[7] After Gilgit was leased to the British, the State forces stationed at Gilgit were withdrawn to Bunji on the left bank of the Indus and 35 miles South of Gilgit Cantonment. A local force called 'Gilgit Scouts' on the pattern of Frontier Guides led by British officers was raised in

Gilgit to consolidate British authority in the region.[8] The announcement of Independence however, forced the British to hand over the Gilgit Agency back to the Maharaja rather prematurely.

With the lapse of paramountcy in 1947, British Indian Government handed over the administrative control of all areas of the Gilgit Agency, including Hunza, to the Kashmir State Government.[9] Accordingly, Brigadier Ghansar Singh was appointed by the Maharaja as the Governor of these areas on July 19, 1947. He was till then the Brigadier General Staff of the State Forces and his appointment as governor was against the wishes of Ram Chandra Kak, the then Prime Minister of the State. Brigadier Ghansar Singh arrived in Gilgit on July 30, 1947 along with Major-General Scott, the Commander-in-Chief of Kashmir State Forces. During their meeting with Major Brown, the Commandant of Gilgit Scouts, "Subedar Major Babar Khan and all the JCOs clearly stated that they would serve the State, if their demands are accepted".[10] The demands primarily related to the service conditions of the troops. The next day all civil officers met him and informed him that they would serve the state only if their salaries were increased.[11] On his own initiative before leaving Srinagar, the Governor had asked Raja Noor Ali Khan, the then Revenue Assistant at Astor and Captain Durga Singh, Company Commander 5th Kashmir Infantry Battalion to meet him at Gilgit.

When Ghansar Singh took over the administration from Lt Col Beacon, the political agent on August 1, 1947, the entire office work of the administration came to a grinding halt. This was because all the British officers had opted for Pakistan and the replacements from the State though appointed had still not arrived. The civil establishment in Gilgit had refused to serve till they were guaranteed higher rates of pay. It appeared that both the Gilgit Scouts and the local as well as non-local civil employees had adopted an "attitude of non-cooperation" with the Governor "at the instigation of some of the British officers." To compound matters all the controlled stores had been spent or distributed and not even "an ounce of sugar" or "a yard of cloth" was left in the stores. General Scott returned to Srinagar on August 2, 1947 with a promise to get some assistance. He carried with him the demands put both by the Gilgit Scouts and civilian officials regarding improvement of their service conditions.[12]

For the next three months the Governor was a lame duck. He sent regular communications to the authorities at Srinagar informing them about the state of affairs in Gilgit and surrounding areas and requesting immediate assistance. However, palace intrigues at Srinagar ensured that these correspondences rarely fetched a reply and accordingly no tangible help came from Srinagar to bolster the Maharaja's administration in Gilgit. Even General Scott's attempts to highlight the situation in Gilgit fell on deaf ears. It seems as if the Maharaja's administration was too preoccupied by internal intrigues and the problems in Poonch and the valley to spare thoughts and resources for a far-flung region. Militarily no attempts were made to significantly consolidate the Maharaja's hold in Gilgit agency. One company of 5th Jammu and Kashmir Infantry commanded by Captain Durga Singh and located at Bunji 34 miles short of Gilgit was replaced by 6th Jammu and Kashmir Infantry comprising two companies each of Sikh and Muslim troops and led by Lieutenant Colonel Abdul Majeed Khan. Services of some British Officers had been retained by the State and consequently a 500-strong contingent of Gilgit Scouts was commanded by Major William Brown, who was assisted by another British officer Captain Jock Matheson, besides Captain Mohammad Sayeed Durrani and Lieutenant Ghulam Haider of Kashmir State Army. "During this period, Muslim Officers of the State army had contacted the Scout Officers and decided to establish Pakistan in Gilgit".[13]

2nd and 4th Jammu and Kashmir Infantry of Jammu and Kashmir State Forces had participated in the Second World War and had proved their mettle. Captain Mirza Hassan Khan and Captain Mohammad Aslam of 4th Jammu and Kashmir Infantry were awarded Military Cross. "During this period Mirza Hassan Khan along with other Muslim officers met Qaid-e-Azam in Bombay and sought his guidance". After the Second World War, some of the Muslim officers of the State Forces got together and hatched a secret Military Revolutionary Council. This was headed by "Mirza Hassan Khan and it initially included Major Afzal Shaheed, Major Mohammad Din, Major Rehmat Ullah, Major Sher, Major Ghazanfar Ali Shah, Major Feroz Din, and Captain Mansha". They succeeded in indoctrinating a large number of uneducated Muslim JCOs and other ranks. However, almost all senior serving Muslim officers and a large number of other Muslim officers did not join them in this conspiracy. Although the information about the conspiracy had leaked and the authorities were aware of Hassan Khan's political leanings, no action was initiated against him, to avoid precipitating matters. Meanwhile, he had moved to the 6th Battalion of the State Forces and was shifted to far-flung Bunji, to relieve a company of 5th Jammu and Kashmir Rifles commanded by Captain Durga Singh. It was initially intended to dispose off a troublesome officer to a remote corner and the rest of the battalion was to remain at Nowshera. "This was prudent especially in the wake of the troubled state of affairs of the state and fact that out of a total of nine Battalions of the state Army, almost one Battalion was already looking after the peaceful Northern regions".[14]

Hassan Khan left Srinagar on September 1, 1947 and reached Bunji on September 10, 1947 and occupied upper quarters.[15] During their movement to Bunji, Hassan Khan and his troops are reported to have raised pro-Pakistan slogans, which were brought to the notice of the Governor and who promptly reported the same to Major General Scott and Brigadier Rajinder Singh, who had taken over as the Brigadier General Staff. Scott had already received similar reports from the State police and had directed that the culprits be arrested and sent to Srinagar under escort. He also sent a message to

Mirza Hassan Khan directing him to report back immediately, which was totally ignored. After realising the gravity of the situation, taking into account the aggressive posture of Hassan Khan and his troops, and total inadequacy of force available at Gilgit to neutralise it, the 6th Jammu and Kashmir Infantry Battalion stationed at Nowshera was directed to immediately rush to Srinagar. After it reached Srinagar it was dispatched to Bunji.[16] The first element of the 6th Battalion to reach Bunji was 'C' Company led by Captain Nek Alam, who according to Hassan Khan had pro-Congress leanings. The Company occupied the lower quarters at Bunji. The rest of the battalion led by Lieutenant Colonel Abdul Majeed Khan Durrani reached Bunji by the fourth week of September 1947. The "Battalion comprised of five companies: A and B Companies had Sikh and Dogra Sepoys under the command of Captain Baldeo Singh and Captain Sukh Deo Singh respectively while C and D Companies had all Muslims under the command of Captain Nek Alam and Captain Hassan Khan respectively". Captain Parmut Singh was in charge of administration and commanded the Headquarter Company which had sepoys of all communities. Later, Major Ehsan Ali was posted in to relieve Captain Parmut Singh. "One Sikh company of this battalion was posted to Laiyya in Ladakh". On arrival of the battalion at Bunji, Captain Nek Alam with a platoon was sent to Skardu allegedly at the behest of Hassan Khan for his pro-Gandhi leanings, to relieve Major Ehsan Ali, who had shown his pro-Pakistan leanings. However, the other two platoons of his company "under the command of Subedar Mohammad Ali remained in Bunji".[17]

After Lieutenant Colonel Majeed Khan reached Bunji, he telephonically informed the Governor that on enquiry, "he had found that there was no truth in allegations against Hassan Khan and only religious slogans had been shouted". The report was subsequently sent to the Chief of Staff through the Governor. During this period Hassan Khan contacted elements within Gilgit Scouts "to establish Pakistan in Gilgit".[18] Captain

Saeed Durrani, the Second-in-Command of Gilgit Scouts, has reportedly mentioned in his memoirs that Hassan Khan took from him an oath of allegiance on holy Quran whilst on a trout fishing trip in Kargah Nullah near Gilgit. The others, who subsequently took the "oath of the secret military council on Quran" to topple the Maharaja's government, included Captain Muhammad Khan, the Quarter Master, Lieutenant Ghulam Haider the Adjutant and Subedar Major Babar Khan of Gilgit Scouts. Babar Khan subsequently submitted "a written oath of allegiance from responsible key personnel of Scouts to Captain Saeed Durrani", who was acting as "Deputy of the Military Revolutionary Council, headed by Hassan Khan, whose orders were to be obeyed at all cost". Although, Subedar Major Babar Khan's account differs slightly from that of Capt Saeed in that he has recorded that Hassan Khan had taken both him and Saeed Durrani to Naikoi water channel tunnel South of Gilgit and took an oath on Quran to topple the Maharaja's rule, it is pertinent to note that the conspiracies to topple the government had started much before Maharaja Hari Singh declared accession of the State of Jammu and Kashmir to India or for that matter its independence. "After Lieutenant Colonel Majeed Khan arrived at Bunji, Hassan Khan cultivated all the Muslim elements of the Regiment and knitted a close web around his Commanding Officer and through them he remained abreast of what all was transpiring between his Commanding Officer and the Governor about his arrest". According to Major Brown the Governor and the Commanding Officer 6th Battalion, in order to avoid aggravating an already serious volcanic situation, got the orders of sending Hassan under arrest annulled.[19]

As far as Gilgit Scouts were concerned it must be appreciated, that it was not a homogenous force. Its different platoons were formed by men from different principalities in the region and owed their allegiance to them. These local rulers wielded considerable influence on the men from their region and all the rulers except the ruler of Chitral continued to profess their loyalty to the Maharaja till the very end. In fact, "Raja of Punial even came to defend Brigadier Ghansara Singh with his body guards", when he was subsequently attacked.[20] Besides, there were serious differences along sectarian and ethnic lines amongst troops of Gilgit Scouts. Moreover, Gilgit Scouts was basically a militia, which was lightly armed and incapable of taking on State forces, which were better armed. The apolitical nature of Gilgit Scouts is clearly evident from their 12 point charter of demands submitted to Ghansar Singh. Its contents relate only to pay and service conditions and nowhere does it talk about Pakistan or any other religious factor.[21] Now, if at that period the Scouts had intended to revolt in three months time against the Kashmir regime, it is most unlikely that they would have submitted these requests, most of which are in connection with long-term benefits such as pensions and gratuities. Moreover Gilgit Scouts as well as local population were "free from the violent communal passions that were sweeping through Punjab".[22] In fact, this was the main reason why the Governor subsequently chose Gilgit Scouts over Muslim troops of 6th Jammu and Kashmir Infantry, who were mainly from Jammu region to defend Gilgit. The fact is that most elements from Gilgit Scouts were sitting on the fence and joined the rebels after they were led to believe that Srinagar had fallen to the tribal raiders.

After Pakistan invaded Jammu and Kashmir and the Maharaja fled Srinagar for Jammu and acceded to India there was pandemonium in Gilgit. Rumours were floating that Srinagar had fallen and conspiracies were being hatched by the Gilgit Scouts and elements of State forces. An alarmed non-Muslim population approached the Governor and requested him to send for army detachments from Bunji. The Governor advised them to remain in Gilgit and face whatever was in store for them. "The Governor was in a fix. He had to weigh the two alternatives" namely the Gilgit Scouts and the 6th Jammu and Kashmir Infantry and after weighing the merits and demerits of both the options, he decided to bank on Gilgit Scouts. On October 30, 1947, he had a telephonic conversation with Lieutenant Colonel Majeed Khan at Bunji and "ordered him to reach Gilgit with as large a force as he could muster". However, in the early hours of November 1, 1947, just after midnight, the house of the Governor was surrounded by about 100 Scouts. They demanded that he surrender. The Governor surrendered ostensibly with a view to protect the lives of non-Muslim residents. The surrender, however, led to the disintegration of State Forces, with troops killing each other. Most of the Sikh troops were killed; the others ran away to the mountains to save their lives.[23] After the Governor's arrest a provisional government of 'People's Republic of Gilgit and Baltistan' was set up.[24] It was headed by a local, Rais Khan and included Major Brown, Captain Ehsan Ali, Captain Hassan (both of State Forces), Captain Sayeed, Lieutenant Haider (both on secondment from State Forces to Gilgit Scouts), Subedar Major Babar Khan (of Gilgit scouts) and Wazir Wilayat Ali. It must be noted that none of the local Rajas were included in the Provisional Government.[25] On November 4, 1947, the Pakistani flag was hoisted at the Gilgit Scouts lines by Major Brown.[26] Brown later described his action as a 'coup d' etat' and informed Sir George Cunningham, the new Governor of the NWFP at Peshawar about the accession of Gilgit to Pakistan, who directed him to restore order in the region.[27] Subsequently, the rulers of the enclaves of Hunza and Nagar, within the Gilgit Agency, which were vassals of the Maharaja of Kashmir also declared their accession to Pakistan.

As regards the role of Major Brown, who subsequently claimed credit for bringing the region to Pakistan and was posthumously awarded Star of Pakistan by Pakistani government. A careful analysis will indicate that he joined the rebels only as a last resort. He and Captain Matheson, another British officer were "retained in the State Army, on their own consent and thus in accordance with the rules/ regulations they were directly responsible to Governor Ghansar Singh. As per a debriefing report of Major Brown, he used to daily present the facts before Governor". He took steps to prevent the rebellion and tried to disperse the rebel elements. As soon as he and Captain Matheson realized that an underground movement was at work, he posted Captain Saeed to Misgar/ Kalanderchi Fort near Chinese border; Captain Muhammad Khan Jaral was posted from Gilgit Scouts to 6th Jammu and Kashmir Infantry at Bunji; "Subedar Raja Jan Alam Nagri based at Chilas in Gilgit Scouts was dismissed from service; Subedar Major Raja Babar Khan was mostly kept on patrolling and was about to be discharged".[28] Major Brown also tried to protect the lives of non-Muslim population and was arrested twice by the rebels in the initial days of rebellion but after Pakistani authority was established, he not only re-established his authority over Gilgit Scouts but also took credit for transferring the region to Pakistan. Major Brown has "tried to conceal his real terms of services" with the Maharaja of Kashmir in his book, 'The Gilgit Rebellion'.[29] It suited both Indian and Pakistani historians to assign him pre-eminence in the events that took place in Gilgit. For Pakistanis it was essential to show that Gilgit Scouts were at the forefront in the rebellion against the Maharaja to portray the revolt as indigenous—the spin given was that Major Brown was moved to action on account of strong sentiments in favour of Pakistan amongst his troops, who were local inhabitants. From India's point of view his involvement indicated British complicity and supported various conspiracy theories.

"General chaos and lawlessness prevailed in the entire Gilgit region for the next few days" after the surrender by the Governor and there was large scale massacre of Hindus and Sikhs who refused to convert. It must, however, be noted that "the Amirs, Rajas and the people of Gilgit in general had no hand in revolt or the atrocities that were perpetrated on the minority community".[30]

After the capture of Dardistan, next step was the invasion of Baltistan. This was led by Major Ehsan Ali and included troops from 6th Kashmir Light Infantry, Gilgit Scouts and about 1200 combatants from Chitral sent by the *Mehtar* of Chitral.[31] Baltistan was part of Ladakh district and ruled by a Wazir-i-Wazarat on behalf of the Maharaja who would stay six months in Skardu, three months in Kargil and three months in Laiyya. He was not only responsible for maintaining law and order, but also for collecting revenue as well as dispensing justice. From 1899 onwards "one platoon with 50 men under a Major or Captain was posted" at Skardu and in "Kharpocha Fort 11 men manned two guns".[32] In 1947, Amar Nath was the Wazir-i-Wazarat of Ladakh and Skardu. He realised that Pakistani agents were not really succeeding in subverting the population in Ladakh, which was overwhelmingly Buddhist, and Kargil, which was still under Buddhist influence, but Skardu "due to its mostly illiterate Muslim population" could be "easy prey for the enemy agents". He thus realised that Skardu was probably the weakest link which could possibly be severed by the enemy. He, therefore, ordered that administrative headquarters of the district be shifted to Skardu. He also "selected sites for airports at Ladakh, Kargil and Skardu", to bring in the army in times of an emergency.[33] He also called a meeting of the leading citizens and local rulers "to ascertain their mind and to remind them of their oath of allegiance" to the Maharaja. One of the local rulers, Raja of Rondu, who was known to be in touch with Pakistan, did not attend the meeting. Only one of the rulers, Raja of Khaplu was loyal to the Maharaja; rest were opportunist and would support any one who emerged winner. Amar Nath then ordered the "confiscation of all the guns and ammunition lying with them".[34]

"In July 1947, one platoon of the C Company of the 6th Battalion of Kashmir State Army, consisting of fifty men was sent to Skardu under the command of Major Mohammad Din. His second-in-command was Captain Krishan Singh" but Major Mohammad Din was secretly working for Pakistan and when the information was divulged, "he was transferred on October 15, 1947" and replaced by "Captain Nek Alam from Bunji". From Laiyya, Major Sher Jang Thapa was promoted as Lieutenant Colonel and "transferred to Skardu along with Captain Ganga Singh and 85 Sikh soldiers".[35] Lieutenant Colonel Thapa, who had become the garrison commander of Ladakh and Skardu, arrived in Skardu on December 3, 1947. Until then the troops of 6th Battalion, who were guarding this region, had an overwhelming majority of Muslims. Captain Nek Alam who was commanding them had proved his loyalty on a number of occasions and had even handed over two letters written by Hassan Khan inciting Muslim troops at Skardu to revolt.[36] Lieutenant Colonel Thapa on arrival surveyed the area and wanted to withdraw to Kargil along with the civil administration to set up a firm base there and patrol up to Skardu but Wazir-i-Wazarat did not approve of his plans. In fact he wanted Lieutenant Colonel Thapa to set up defences at Stak 70 miles from Skardu and on the border with Gilgit.[37] Lieutenant Colonel Thapa eventually "selected Tsari 20 miles North West of Skardu" towards Rondu to set up his defensive line as it had steep hills on two sides and the River Indus in between. "He deputed two platoons to guard this bottleneck"; one led by Captain Nek Alam on the far bank and other by Captain Krishan Singh to defend the near bank.[38]

In the meantime the local population was being subverted and seeing the rebels gain ground, had started turning hostile, but, a low level flight by two Indian aircraft on a reconnaissance mission in December 1947 "terrorised the Baltis" and softened their attitude. However, no efforts were made to land any aircraft at Skardu with the aim of proving the landing strip.[39] In January 1948 the Pakistanis launched Ibex Force led by Major Ehsan Ali to capture Baltistan. "The force gathered together at Harmaush" on January 29, 1948 and reached Istak on February 4. To meet the invaders Thapa sent two sections under Captain Ganga Singh but as they were advancing towards Rondu some of the Muslim soldiers who had already been subverted, and "were on patrolling duty sabotaged the whole action by mutual firing" and Captain Ganga Singh was forced to return to Skardu.[40] Meanwhile, Captain Nek Alam was arrested by Muslim soldiers and "when Major Ehsan Ali reached Tsari, Captain Nek Alam was presented to him and he agreed to work with them". Along with him 32 Muslim soldiers also joined the rebels.[41] Throughout the campaign in Gilgit-Baltistan, many loyal Muslim officers when captured, agreed to work for the enemy. Their decisions were governed partly by self preservation and partly by the fact that the rebels were on the ascendancy then. The only notable exception to the rule was Lieutenant Colonel Majeed Khan, the Commanding Officer of the 6th Battalion of Jammu and Kashmir Infantry.

On the night of February 8/9, the outpost at Tsari already weakened by the desertion of Muslim troops, was attacked. All the troops of "Sikh platoon under Captain Krishan Singh were either killed in action or murdered after being captured". The first batch of reinforcement of 90 men led by Captain Prabhat Singh reached Skardu on February 10 and in the early hours of February 11, "Skardu Cantonment was encircled and attacked by around 600 men" armed with 3" and 2" mortars, Medium Machine Guns (MMG), Light Machine Guns (LMG) and rifles.[42] A plot had been hatched to take possession of the Quarter Guard and cantonment with the help of Muslim troops, who not only deserted and opened the gates of the cantonment for raiders but also latched the doors of barracks where non-Muslim troops were staying from outside. However, prudent actions by Lieutenant Colonel Thapa and his troops prevented the cantonment from falling into enemy hands and the raiders led by Major Ehsan Ali were forced to withdraw. However, Wazir along with some other Hindu and Sikh officials were killed and the treasury, which was being guarded by Muslim troops, was looted. By the night of February 11, every single Hindu and Sikh at Skardu, which included a large number of women and children, had taken shelter in the cantonment. On February 13, the second batch of reinforcement of 70 soldiers led by Lieutenant Ajai Singh reached Skardu. However, by the end of February the raiders were occupying positions all around Skardu and also the tactically important Point 8853 (Khari Dong), the highest point on Kharpocha Hill on the South Bank of Indus overlooking the cantonment and entire Skardu town.[43]

A subsequent attempt to reinforce Skardu by Brigadier Faqir Singh ended in disaster as this convoy was ambushed at Thergo just 16 km from Skardu and forced to retreat by rebels.[44] The state forces led by Lieutenant Colonel Sher Jung Thapa continued to defend Skardu gallantly for over six months, despite being totally cut off from rest of the Indian forces. The rebels kept closing their circle and by early April 1948, Skardu Garrison had an area of not more than 1,500 yards by 600 yards. All supplies of ration from the town were cut off.[45] Another attempt to reinforce Skardu Garrison by a relatively strong force led by Colonel Kripal Singh also ended in disaster.[46] However, the fierce resistance and the will to fight exhibited by Skardu Garrison forced the enemy to bypass Skardu and move forward. The rebels supported by Pakistani forces captured Zojila Pass in May 1948 and infiltrated through Drass, Kargil, and other points to threaten Leh. Indian Army had to subsequently use tanks to clear them from Zojila and defend Leh.[47] It was indeed ironic that despite the heroic resistance put up by Thapa and his troops, the Indian Armed forces could not relieve Skardu and assist the garrison there. The Army's efforts to link up with the garrison were foiled by the infiltrators who ambushed the two columns that had been sent to relieve the garrison at Skardu; the Air Force for some inexplicable reasons was reluctant to undertake supply missions to Skardu by Dakotas,[48] although they undertook far more risky operations during the war. "By its wonderful exploits at Poonch and Leh, the RIAF had set itself a standard of performance which unfortunately could not be maintained at Skardu".[49] The Air Force did airdrop some supplies but they fell far short of the minimum needs of the besieged garrison and the non-Muslim population that had taken refuge in the cantonment.[50] According to Skumar Mahajan, son of deceased Wazir Amar Nath, the first Indian aircraft to make appearance over Skardu after the siege of Skardu started in February, did so on June 19, 1948. The aircraft did boost the morale but as the aircraft were Tempest fighters it was impossible for them "to maintain the garrison, which required a daily ration of 800 lbs plus ammunition".[51] "Unable to break the resistance of Skardu garrison", the Pakistanis "brought into action 3.7" Howitzers on August 9" and started shelling the garrison. Already crippled by the lack of rations and ammunition, Skardu garrison led by Lieutenant Colonel Sher Jung Thapa eventually crumbled under the heavy shelling and surrendered on August 14, 1948. With the surrender of Skardu Garrison the control over Baltistan and surrounding areas passed on to Pakistan.[52]

An analysis of events of 1947-48 in Gilgit-Baltistan clearly highlights that it were the subverted troops of Jammu and Kashmir Infantry who were instrumental in bringing this region under Pakistani occupation. Almost all of these troops were from outside the region (mainly from Jammu region of the state), who were subsequently joined by Pakistani regulars during the attack on Baltistan. Another significant component of the rebel forces was the buttress provided by Mehtar of Chitral. Although Gilgit Scouts and some locals joined them, most did so for self preservation and to flow with the tide. The local population generally remained aloof but always supported whoever was stronger at that point.

Notes.

[1] The region along with much of present day Jammu and Kashmir was part of the Kushana Empire as well as Emperor Lalitaditya's (724 – 761 AD) kingdom. Subsequently Sultan Shihabuddin (1354 -1373), Sultan Zain-ul-abidin (1420-1470) and Ghazi Shah (1561-63) not only ruled over Kashmir Valley but also over Gilgit and Skardu. During Mughal period

and during early period of Afghan Rule Baltistan was part of Kashmir, though Dardic territory remained out of it.

2   FM Hassnain, *Gilgit: The Northern Gate of India*, New Delhi: Sterling Publishers Pvt Ltd, 1978, p 27.

3   Prithivi Nath Kaul Bamzai, *A History of Kashmir*, New Delhi: Metropolitan Book Company, 1973, p 619.

4   Ibid, p 675.

5   NN Raina, *Kashmir Politics and Imperialist Manoeuvres 1846 – 1980*, New Delhi: Patriot Publishers, 1988, p 103.

6   Amar Singh Chohan, *The Gilgit Agency 1877-1935*, New Delhi: Atlantic Publishers & Distributors, p 220.

7   Ahmad Hasan Dani, *History of Northern Areas of Pakistan*, Islamabad: National Institute of Historical and Cultural Research, 1991, p 298. Also see Hassnain no 2, pp 140-141.

8   Balraj Madhok, *A story of Bungling in Kashmir*, New Delhi: Young Asia Publications, p 71.

9   Prem Shankar Jha, *Kashmir 1947: Rival Versions of History*, New Delhi: Oxford University Press, 1996, p 7.

10 Hassnain, no. 2, pp 150-152.

11 Dani, no. 7, pp 334 -335

12 Hassnain, no 2. pp 152 -153.

13 Ibid pp 154-155.

14 Balwaristan National Movement Website http:// www.balawaristan.net/GB.html (Accessed on August 16, 2006).

15 Dani, no. 7, p 337.

16 Brigadier Ghansar Singh, *Gilgit before 1947* as sited in Balwaristan National Movement Website http:// www.balawaristan.net/GB.html (Accessed on August 16, 2006).

17 Dani, no. 7, p 337.

18 Hassnain, no. 2. p 155.

[19] Note 14 ibid.

[20] Dani , no. 7, p 327.

[21] Ibid., pp 335 -336.

[22] SN Prasad and Dharam Pal, *History of Operations in Jammu & Kashmir (1947 – 48)*, New Delhi: Ministry of Defence, Government of India, 2005, pp 280 -281.

[23] Hassnain, no. 2, pp 155-157.

[24] P Stobdan, "North West Under The Maharaja" in Jasjit Singh (ed), *Pakistan Occupied Kashmir: Under The Jackboot*, New Delhi: Siddhi Books, 1995, p 41.

[25] Prasad no 22, p 282.

[26] FM Hassnain, no 2, pp 157-158.

[27] Narendra Singh Sarila, *The Shadow of the Great Game: The Untold Story of India's Partition*, New Delhi: Harper Collins Publishers India, 2005, pp 333-334.

[28] Note 14 ibid.

[29] Ibid.

[30] K Brahma Singh, *History of Jammu & Kashmir Rifles (1820 -1956)*, New Delhi: Lancer International, 1990, p 245.

[31] Hassnain, no 2, p 158.

[32] Dani, no 7, p 334.

[33] Skumar Mahajan, *Debacle in Baltistan*, New Delhi, 1973, p 25.

[34] Ibid, p 26.

[35] Dani, no 7., p 338.

[36] Prasad, no 22, p 283.

[37] Mahajan, no 33, p 16.

[38] Dani, no 7, p 378.

[39] Mahajan, no 33, p 39.

[40] Dani, no 7, pp 379-380.

[41] Ibid.

42 Mahajan, no 33, pp 54 -62.

43 Dani, no 7, pp 383-385 and Mahajan, no 33, pp 55-71.

44 Brahma Singh, no 30, p 261.

45 Message by Lt Col Thapa as quoted in Mahajan, no 33, pp 89-90.

46 Brahma Singh, no 30, pp 262 – 263.

47 Jasjit Singh, "Battle for Siachin: Beginning of the Third War" in Jasjit Singh (ed), *Kargil 1999: Pakistan's Fourth War for Kashmir*, New Delhi: Knowledge World, 1999, p 62.

48 PC Lal, *My Years with the IAF*, New Delhi: Lancer International, 1986, pp 64-65.

49 Prasad, no 22, 306.

50 Madhok, no 8, p 73.

51 Mahajan, no 33, pp 109-110.

52 Ibid, pp 124-125.

5

A History of POK— Pakistan Occupied Kashmir[1]

Parvez Dewan

By December 1946 it was quite clear that India was about to become independent of the British, and that it would be divided into two countries when the British left: an avowedly Muslim Pakistan and an India that aspired to be secular.

Jammu and Kashmir's Maharaja Hari Singh and his Prime Minister (Ram Chandra Kak) toyed with the idea of independence.

Kashmir's most popular leader, Sheikh Muhammad Abdullah favoured secular India. However, labour leaders like Pt. Prem Nath Bazaz wanted Kashmir to accede to Pakistan. Till as late as September 1946, the Muslim Conference, which had some hold on the Muslims of Jammu and Poonch, favoured responsible government under the Maharaja, without association with India or Pakistan. And their views had the backing of the founder of Pakistan, Muhammad Ali Jinnah, till almost a month before the partition of India. Even as late as July 11, 1947, Mr. Jinnah was advising the leaders of the Muslim Conference to ask for an independent Kashmir under the Maharaja. (Mr. Jinnah's party, the Muslim League, changed its views only on July 29, barely seventeen days before the creation of Pakistan.)

As a result, the Maharaja was not able to decide either way. So, on August 14/15, 1947, when Pakistan and India became independent, Jammu and Kashmir was one of the only three princely states that had joined neither India nor Pakistan.

The Situation in Poonch

Trouble started in Poonch as soon as the British departed the subcontinent. The region had a large population of ex-servicemen, who had been demobilised after the Second World War. On August 25, 1947 there was a public meeting at Neela Butt (Dherkote) at which some people spoke in favour of Pakistan. Some soldiers of the Maharaja started shooting at the people assembled there.

By August 27, Sardar Abdul Qaiyum Khan, a former army sepoy, had assembled a band of militants. Sardar Ibrahim, who was one of the main anti-India leaders, crossed over to Pakistan and sought the support of the Pakistan Army to sustain the rebellion.

The Three-fold Strategy of the Pakistan Army

Pakistan grew impatient with the impasse in Jammu and Kashmir. It assumed that Jammu and Kashmir belonged to Pakistan because of the state's Muslim majority.

Pakistan's army drew up a three-fold plan to annex the state.

i) **The Border Areas:** Pakistan first sent armed soldiers—perhaps four thousand[2]—to sneak into Jammu province, all the way from Mirpur in the north-west to Kathua in the south-east.

ii) **Poonch:** Undivided Poonch had a martial history unlike any other district of undivided India. So, Pakistan persuaded Sardar Mohammad Ibrahim Khan of Poonch to organise a force of veterans from the

British Army and deserters from the Maharaja's forces. The veterans alone numbered sixty thousand.[3] Pakistan launched this part of its plan on August 23, 1947, when terrorists under its command killed Jagat Ram, the magistrate of Rawlakot (Poonch).

iii) *The Valley of Kashmir:* On October 22, 1947,[4] Pakistan sent thousands of Afridi tribesmen—thirty thousand according to Mr. Maini[5]—into the state. They were led by Maj. (Retd.) Khurshid Anwar.

Lt. Col. (later Maj. Gen.) Akbar Khan headed this three-pronged operation. His *nom de guerre* was Gen. Tariq.

The Pakistani Invasion

Khushdil Khan of Mardan (NWFP) collected the 'lashkar' (armed force) of tribesmen. The Pakistan Army put them in trucks and took them to Batrasi, north-east of Abbottabad, which is on the Kashmir border.

By October 15, the tribals drove the Maharaja's forces out of Fort Owen. Maj. Amin adds that 'around the same time the Dogra communication between Kotli and Poonch was severed and the state forces' Muslim troops had almost *deserted* and joined the rebels while the non-Muslim units were besieged at Bhimber, Mirpur and Mangla.' (Emphasis added.) The Dogra force was also besieged at Bagh, Mendhar and Poonch in Jammu province.

The Maharaja's force had a miniscule, and mostly ceremonial, presence in these areas. (His *entire* force consisted of nine infantry battalions.) Most of the Maharaja's soldiers had never faced a war—only the few who had volunteered to assist the Allies in the Second World War had. On the other side was the army of the fourth biggest country in the world—with many distinguished veterans of the Second World War. The Maharaja's soldiers started fleeing the villages for the towns.

A band of two thousand 'tribesmen captured the bridge spanning the Neelam river on the Hazara Trunk Road linking Muzaffarabad with Abbottabad *without a fight* (on the night of October 20/21) since the all-Muslim guard platoon of 4th Jammu and Kashmir Infantry joined the tribesmen,...[5] (Emphasis added).

The Instrument of Accession

On October 15, 1947, the Pakistani 'irregulars' overran Fort Owen, seized Muzaffarabad on October 21 and were in Baramulla on October 26.

The Maharaja had thitherto been trying to keep the state independent of both India and Pakistan. Now he realised that this 'third option' was no longer available. He asked his Deputy Prime Minister, Mr. Batra, to rush to Delhi to ask India to send in its army. The Government of India did not oblige. It wanted some kind of a constitutional link with Kashmir before it sent in its troops.

It was on October 26, 1947, that Maharaja Hari Singh signed the Instrument of Accession. This Instrument gave the 'dominion legislature' (later, the Parliament of India) the power to 'make laws for this state' only with respect to matters concerning defence, external affairs, communications and some ancillary matters. There was a proviso that the final disposition of the state of Jammu and Kashmir would be made by the free will of the people, as soon as law and order was restored.

October-November 1947: Pakistan annexes considerable territory in Jammu

Major Boston[6] and Capt. Feroz of the Pakistan Army were the heroes of their side. They soon annexed Trar Khail, Devi Gali and Hijayr. Pakistan then seized Mirpur, Bhimber and Deva Batala.

The anti-India militia assaulted camps of the Maharaja's forces and police at Dherkote/Dhirkot and killed a number of Dogra personnel.

On October 24, 1947, a 'government' was constituted for the areas occupied by Pakistan. Trar Khail (Palandri) was its first 'capital.' Sardar Mohammad Ibrahim Khan was installed as its 'President.'

Meanwhile, the Pakistani forces annexed Bhimber, Mirpur, Kotli, Mendhar, Naushera and Rajouri. (The Indian Army liberated the last three areas later.)

'Azad Jammu and Kashmir,' too, loses its '*azadi*' (freedom)

After Pakistan occupied Mirpur, Muzaffarabad-'Neelum' valley and parts of Poonch-Rajouri, it officially established the Government of '*Azad*' ('free') Jammu and Kashmir' ('AJK') on October 4, 1947.

In theory, 'AJK' was a free land and not part of Pakistan. Quaid e Azam Muhammad Ali Jinnah, the founder of Pakistan did not want Pakistan to forcibly annex Jammu and Kashmir. He wanted to leave the matter to the Kashmiris to decide.

Mr. Anwar became the first 'President' of this region. His provisional presidency lasted twenty-one days (October 4, 1947-October 24, 1947).

The Pakistan Government then installed Sardar Mohammad Ibrahim Khan of the Muslim Conference as the President of 'AJK'. Ibrahim was rewarded for blocking his own party's move to pass a resolution asking for independence from Pakistan.

Sardar Ibrahim Khan became the founder president of the 'Azad Jammu and Kashmir' government "when many veterans like Mirwaiz Yusuf Shah had blatantly refused to head the interim set-up.[7]" He spoke for Pakistan at the United Nations in 1948 when discussions on Kashmir came up.

Chaudhary Ghulam Abbas reaches 'AJK' (POK)

In February 1948, Sheikh Abdullah, who was the Prime Minister of the Indian state of Jammu and Kashmir, released Chaudhary Ghulam Abbas from jail, and allowed him to cross over to 'AJK'.

The Sheikh asked the Chaudhary to try to get the Pakistan government to agree to tripartite talks between the leaders of India, Pakistan and Kashmir. Mr Jinnah rejected the idea— perhaps because, like his Indian counterparts, he considered Kashmir a bipartite issue with India alone. (Both countries follow this line partly because the Indian Independence Act, 1947, does not accept any third nation, province or state as a successor state to British India.)

Instead, an agreement was arrived at between the Pakistan Government and the Muslim Conference (MC) on April 28, 1949. M.A. Gurmani, Minister without Portfolio, signed on behalf of the Government of Pakistan. Sardar Mohammad Ibrahim, 'President', signed for 'Azad Jammu and Kashmir' and Chaudhary Ghulam Abbas for the All-J&K MC, of which he was the President. Under this accord the MC is required to look after Pakistan's interests not only in the Pakistan occupied territory but also in the part actually administered by India.

This came to be known as the Karachi Agreement. It gave Pakistan temporary administrative control over the occupied territories.

Worse, it hived Gilgit-Baltistan (which Pakistan calls the 'Northern Areas') off from 'Azad Jammu and Kashmir' and gave Pakistan direct control over this huge region. This cynical decimation of its territory is the biggest trauma that 'AJK' has suffered in its entire existence.

Neither of the 'Kashmiri' signatories was from Gilgit-Baltistan (or even from the Valley of Kashmir). Two Jammuites, thus, bartered away the destinies of the people of Gilgit-Baltistan, whose representatives were not even consulted.

However, in fairness, Sardar Ibrahim and Chaudhary Abbas had specified that what they were ceding to Pakistan was only for a while.

Trouble in 'AJK'

After Chaudhary Abbas crossed over to 'AJK', he was, naturally, offended to find his junior, Sardar Ibrahim Khan, presuming to be the President of the occupied region. He started persuading Mr Liaquat Ali Khan, the leader of Pakistan, to remove Sardar Ibrahim from the highest office in 'AJK'.

At the time 'AJK' was governed by Rules of Business—a substitute of sorts for a constitution. These rules laid down that the President of 'AJK' could hold his office only during the pleasure of the General Council of the Muslim Conference. Ch. Ghulam Abbas was the President of the MC. Mr. Abbas used the power that the Rules gave him to remove Sardar Ibrahim from his post. (The Sardar's first stint lasted from October 24, 1947 to May 30, 1950.)

Ibrahim retaliated "by threatening to form a parallel Government.[8]"

The Sudhans' revolt, martial law and direct control by Pakistan

The Sudhans a pre-eminent tribe of the region and, all Poonchis, have a long martial tradition. They revolted against the Lahore-based Sikh empire twice—in the 1830s and in 1847. More than 20,000 Poonchis served in the Indian Army in World War I. The number tripled during World War II. These British army veterans were pro-Pakistan in the early years (1947-1950). It is interesting to note that their descendants have been overtly unhappy with Pakistani administration ever since.

Things went wrong in 1950 when Sardar Ibrahim who was a Poonchi, was dismissed. The Sudhans rose in armed revolt. Pakistani forces opened fire on the Sudhan-led agitators. Some Sudhans died in the firings. This incensed the community further. Pakistan imposed martial law on 'AJK' in order to control the situation.

In March 1950, the Pakistan Army rushed its 160 Brigade "to deal with Sardar Ibrahim, who had a large following among the local Sudhan tribes." Pakistan's 25 Brigade replaced it in July. In turn, the 100 Brigade took over in September. (The quote and the dates are from *Pakistan Army—War 1965,* a semi-official but fairly honest Pakistani military history. It would thus be seen that the Army was sent in a good two months before—and obviously in preparation of—Sardar Ibrahim's dismissal.)

The Army decided that the best way to crush this brave martial community was to humiliate it. Soldiers went from house to house—entering bedrooms and ladies' chambers— to flush the Sudhan warriors out.

All this resulted in the secession of the Sudhans from 'AJK'. They set up a parallel government, which was crushed through police action in 1954. Using this as a pretext Pakistan brought 'AJK' under its direct control.

Rapid turnover of 'Presidents'

Being an old-world type of South Asian leader, Chaudhary Abbas thought it beneath his dignity to move into an office that his junior had held. So he got a protege from Mirpur, Sayyed Ali Ahmed Shah, an army veteran, installed as President (May 30, 1950 to December 2, 1951). Abbas gave himself a designation that was higher still: Supreme Head. (Chaudhary Abbas was the 'Supreme Head' of 'AJK' from January 8, 1951 till almost the end of the year.)

This irked Mirwaiz Muhammad Yusuf Shah. He parted ways with both the government and the Muslim Conference. Other members of the MC (by now renamed the 'AJK' MC) were equally unhappy with Chaudhary. They persuaded the

Government of Pakistan to sack him, abolish the post of Supreme Head and make Mirwaiz the head of 'AJK'.

Mirwaiz lasted less than half a year (December 2, 1951 to May 18, 1952). He rubbed a powerful Pakistani civil servant the wrong way. This cost him his job. (His designation had been 'acting Administrator' rather than 'President'.)

Raja Mohammad Haidar Khan (May 18, 1952 to June 21, 1952) was the 'President' for a month or so. Col. Sher Muhammad (or Ahmad) Khan, another army veteran, was the next President (June 21, 1952 to May 30, 1956). However, he was not Chaudhary Ghulam Abbas's man. Abbas persuaded the then Prime Minister of Pakistan, Chaudhary Muhammad Ali (1955–Sept 1956), to sack the Colonel and replace him with Sardar Abdul Qaiyum Khan instead.

However, Mirwaiz had another stint as the 'acting Administrator' for a few months from May 30, 1956 to September 8, 1956 before Sardar Abdul Qaiyum Khan of the 'AJK' Muslim Conference could become the President (September 8, 1956 to April 13, 1957) for a brief while.

The next Prime Minister of Pakistan, Hussain Shaheed Surahwardy, was not happy with his predecessor's choice. He, therefore, changed the 'AJK' leadership. Sardar Mohammad Ibrahim Khan had his second innings as President from April 13, 1957 to April 27, 1959.

Every subsequent change of regime in Pakistan thus saw the 'President' (and, later, Prime Minister) of 'AJK' being replaced. The top official in 'AJK' has, as a result been an appointee of the Government of Pakistan, rather than an elected representative of the people of 'AJK'.

Meanwhile, Field Marshal Ayub Khan took over the Government of Pakistan. Naturally, he wanted his own men to head 'AJK'.

Mr Khurshid Hassan Khurshid became the next President of 'AJK' from May 1, 1959 to August 7, 1964. Abdul Hamid Khan was the President of 'AJK' from August 7, 1964 to October

7, 1969 and was followed by Abdul Rahman Khan as an interim President from October 7, 1969 to October 30, 1970.

By now 'AJK' had run out of potential leaders. So, a game of musical chairs began. The military leader of Pakistan brought Sardar Qaiyum of the 'AJK' MC back from October 30, 1970 to April 16, 1975.

Shaykh Mansur Masud was the interim President of 'AJK' for a few months from April 16, 1975 to June 5, 1975.

Then, Pakistan's Prime Minister, Zulfiqar Ali Bhutto (1971-77, including a stint as President), brought back Sardar Muhammad Ibrahim as the President of 'AJK'. (June 5, 1975 to October 30, 1978), this being the Sardar's third tenure.

'AJK': Elections—at last (and for brief spells at that)

In June 1975, almost twenty-eight years after its occupation by Pakistan, 'AJK' had its first elections. Abdul Hamid Khan (June 1975–August 1977) became its first Prime Minister. Abdul Rahman Khan (August 1977–Oct 1978) followed, as an acting PM.

However, this experiment with democracy was not to last. Gen. Zia ul Haq (1977–88) sacked Mr. Bhutto in a military coup and appointed Brig. Muhammad Hayat Khan as the President of 'AJK' from October 30, 1978 to February 1, 1983. In October 1978, Zia also abolished the newborn institution of Prime Minister—which remained in abeyance till May 1985.

The 'AJK' Presidency saw a change on February 1, 1983, when Abdul Rahman Khan was brought back as the President for the second time. He held that office till 1985.

In 1985 Sardar Abdul Qaiyum Khan of the 'AJK' MC was back as President for the third time. He continued to hold that post till July 11, 1991. However, he now had a Prime Minister as well: Sardar Sikander Hayat Khan, also of the 'AJK' MC (May 1985–July 1990).

Sardar Abdul Qaiyum is a Dhond Abbasi from Poonch. At that time he believed that 'AJK' should join Pakistan. His views were so unpopular in places like Dadial that the audience at his 1985 election rally started hooting him with venom. A huge contingent of the army had to be called in to protect him and whisk him away from the rally. (His views have changed somewhat since then.)

Section 56 of the 1974 provisional constitution of 'AJK' "authorises Islamabad to sack any government in Muzaffarabad if it is a threat to Pakistan's stand on Kashmir. Islamabad uses this constitutional provision as a sword of Damocles over the head of rulers of ('AJK') to keep them under control."[9]

Prime Minister Mumtaz Rathore of the PPP was one victim of this provision in 1991. But, three years later, when his party was in power in Islamabad but not in 'AJK,' his followers (and those of the then 'AJK' President Sardar Sikander) started pressurising Islamabad to use the same power to dismiss the MC government headed by Qaiyum[10].

The fact that Qaiyum's party, the MC, held 40 of the 48 seats in the Legislative Assembly of 1991 was of no help once the government in Islamabad changed and the PPP came to power there.

Pakistan's dreaded Inter-Service Intelligence (ISI) held Sardar Qaiyum aloft for almost fifty years. He later drew close to Mr Nawaz Sharif of the Pakistan Muslim League, but survived in the 1990s mainly because of ISI's support. When he found that neither a majority in the legislature nor friends in the ISI nor even a private army of *mujahids* ('holy warriors') were helpful in the war of nerves that the PPP—then in power in Islamabad—was playing with him, Qaiyum threatened to "set on fire" all of 'AJK' in case his government was removed through the dreaded Section 56.[11]

It worked. He was allowed to complete his five-year term in office.

The Mangla Dam and the exodus of the bitter Mirpuris.

The Mangla Dam was inaugurated in 1967, near Mirpur. About 250 villages were submerged in the reservoir created by the dam. This provoked the Mirpuris, who already had one foot in Britain, and the people of Kotli to migrate *en masse*. Around half a million (five lakh) people from 'AJK'— mostly from Mirpur and Kotli—now live in Yorkshire, Luton, Bradford and Birmingham in the UK.

This alienated them totally from Pakistan—physically as well as emotionally.

The 1990s: political changes

When General Zia ul Haq ousted Pakistan's Prime Minister Z.A. Bhutto in a military coup in 1977, Sardar Ibrahim happened to be the President of 'AJK.' Out of loyalty to Mr. Bhutto, he refused to work with the military junta. This costed him his job.

However, Mr. Bhutto's daughter, Benazir, was not impressed by this sacrifice. When she became the prime minister of Pakistan she made Raja Mumtaz Hussain Rathore, a junior PPP leader, the Prime Minister of 'AJK'. Sardar Ibrahim felt humiliated by this decision. He resigned from the PPP and started his own political group. Rathore was the Prime Minister from July 1990 to July 1991.

In June 1991, Prime Minister Raja Mumtaz Hussain Rathore of PPP refused to accept the results of what he called 'massively rigged elections'[12] For daring to speak out against the Pakistan establishment, he was bodily removed from the office of Prime Minister and shunted to a Rawalpindi jail. This was done under the aforesaid Section 56 of the 1974 Provisional Constitution of 'AJK,' which allows the Government of Pakistan to sack any government in 'AJK' that dares to deviate from the official Pakistani line. It is for reasons like these that it is a cruel joke to call the occupied territory 'azad' (free).

Sardar Muhammad Ashraf (July 5-11, 1991) was the acting PM for a week. Sardar Raja Abdul Qaiyum Khan of the 'AJK' MC (July 1991-July 1996) formally took over as PM from him. Simultaneously, there was a change in the Presidency as well: Sardar Sikander Hayat of the 'AJK' MC (July 1991 to August 25, 1996) assumed that office.

Sardar Ibrahim, Sardar Abdul Qaiyum Khan and K.H. Khurshid were never very happy about the political humiliation of the people of 'AJK' by Pakistan.

A Mirpuri—at last

Sardar Mohammad Ibrahim Khan became the President for a fourth time (August 25, 1996 to August 25, 2001). Sultan Mahmood Chaudhry of PPP was the PM (July 31, 1996 to July 25, 2001). Mahmood was the first Mirpuri to make it to a high position, after five decades of Sudhan-Rajput domination.

The Muslim Conference won 30 of the 48 seats in the State Assembly in July 2001. The party swept the polls because of Sardar Abdul Qaiyum and his son Sardar Atiq. The latter was the president of the party. Twenty-two of the party's legislators were with the father and son duo.

Denying the people representatives of their choosing

The Army felt uneasy at having to deal with leaders with genuine following. Besides, the political stance of Qaiyum and Atiq had rattled the military junta that was then ruling Pakistan.

Qaiyum had, in public statements in London and Muzaffarabad, spoken well of Indian Prime Minister Vajpayee's sincerity to resolve the problem in Kashmir. He had said that Mr Vajpayee's visit to the Minar-e-Pakistan in Lahore in February 1999 was proof that he genuinely wanted peace with Pakistan. Qaiyum condemned the pro-Army Jamaat-e-Islami for using violent *jihadis* in Kashmir. He also came out against Pakistan's insistence that the Hurriyat Conference should be included in negotiations between India and Pakistan about Kashmir. This display of political independence panicked the junta.

So, the Pakistan Army appointed Sardar Sikander Hayat Khan as the Prime Minister of 'AJK' even though (or, perhaps, because) at that time Mr. Khan's position within his own party was shaky.

With the office of 'Prime Minister' gone, Atiq decided to contest for 'President.' The Army pre-empted this by installing an Army man to this post. Maj Gen Mohammed Anwar Khan of Rawalkot was made to resign his commission in the Army. He was rushed to Muzaffarabad where 'Muslim Conference legislators had been ordered to elect him as the President. The legislators were taken aback but could not defy the order."[13]

On July 25, 2001, Maj. Gen. Sardar Sikander Hayat Khan of the 'AJK' MC was sworn in as PM for the second time. Sardar Muhammad Anwar Khan also of the 'AJK' MC, became the President a month later, on August 25, 2001.

A softening of the Line of Control

The year 2005 witnessed major developments. Buses started plying between Muzaffarabad and Srinagar once again after almost six decades. The Governments of India and Pakistan began negotiations about the movement of goods across the LoC. They also agreed to a similar bus service between Poonch (India) and Rawlakote ('AJK').

People began to travel to the other half of the state, again for the first time in ages.

By now the legendary Sardar Abdul Qaiyum Khan was the highest ranking 'AJK' visitor to India. During his longish stay in Delhi he did and said all the right things—from the point of view of bringing peace back to Kashmir and giving realistic advice to the militants. Among other things he said that Kashmir could not become an independent nation in another hundred years. This greatly disappointed Pakistani hardliners.

The earthquake of October 2005

As 2005 drew to a close, nature brought the two halves of Jammu and Kashmir together through its ultimate weapon: grief. The worst earthquake to hit the region since 1885 tore through the state on October 8, 2005.

While the destruction in Uri, Tangdhar and Poonch on the Indian side was terrible (around 1,300 people, including forty-two Indian soldiers, died), 'AJK' was devastated. In a few minutes, more than seventy-three thousand people were killed in 'AJK' and the adjoining areas of Pakistan's Frontier Province.

Thus 'AJK' lost more than two per cent of its population in that earthquake. Maj. Gen. Shaukat Sultan of the Pakistan Army said, "Rawalakot has been destroyed. Muzaffarabad is 70 per cent destroyed. There is not a single family that has not suffered." Balakot and once prosperous Bagh, too were affected very badly. Almost twenty-one lakh (2.1 million) people lost their homes in 'AJK' and the NWFP.

The Indian government agreed to let Pakistani officials pass through Indian territory along the LoC in order to reach AJK's frontier villages affected by the earthquake.

After the quake the Indian soldiers posted on the LoC noticed a sudden lull in the activities of the Pakistan Army. Apart from the loss of three to four hundred soldiers, Pakistani units on the LoC seemed to have lost contact with their headquarters.

One of the Pakistani sentry posts overlooking the Indian Army had collapsed. During that shared tragedy the sentry saw his Indian counterparts not as people who might kill him but as the only comrades he had at that moment. He asked them if they could help him rebuild his watchtower—and they did. They, too, saw the Pakistani sentry as a fellow victim of a terrible calamity and not someone whose tower was meant to keep an eye on their movements.

Quake-hit Pakistani soldiers at the Kaman Post (ahead of Uri) told the Indians that they needed shovels and pickaxes. Once again, the Indians helped. They crossed the Peace Bridge to 'AJK' twice, without weapons, something they would not have even considered a year or two before. They helped the Pakistanis recover their own weapons, which had to be dug out from under the debris.

Pakistani militants rose superbly to the occasion, rescued people and distributed relief materials. And yet, in the July 2006 legislative assembly elections, all 33 candidates of the Muttahida Majlis-e-Amal, an alliance endorsed by the militants, lost. Less surprisingly, the people voted out 13 of the 33 legislators of the ruling 'AJK' MC, including eleven Cabinet ministers. The Peoples Party, which won seven seats, mainly in earthquake-affected Muzaffarabad and Neelum Valley, accused President Musharraf of 'manipulating' the election results. In Narowal it was proved right. The 'AJK' MC, under Sardar Atique Khan, emerged as the biggest party in the 49-member Kashmir legislature. (Eight seats are reserved, five of them for women.)

While the international community did its bit to help the devastated people of 'AJK' and the NWFP, it was felt that it was easier to deliver relief materials from the Indian side.

This change of mood was formalised at Islamabad on October 29, 2005, when India and Pakistan decided to 'open' the Line of Control at five points. These were Chakan da Bagh and Tatta Pani in the Poonch district (Jammu) and Kaman, Haji Pir and Tithwal in the Baramulla and Kupwara districts of Kashmir.

When the first of these points was opened on November 7, 2005, thousands of residents of the devastated Rawalkot area of 'AJK' turned up at the LoC. Their excitement was palpable. The Pakistan Army had to fire tear gas shells to keep them from crossing over to the Indian side.

A few days before, Pakistan's President Gen. Pervez Musharraf had declared that through October 29, 2005 agreement "I have made the LoC irrelevant." While the word 'irrelevant' can be debated, there can be no doubt that the LoC has become softer than at any time since 1965.

Notes

1   The total area of Jammu and Kashmir is 2,22,236 sq. km. Of this the Indian tricolour flies over 45.62 per cent. Pakistan is in the illegal occupation of 35.15 per cent of the state. China has illegally occupied 37,555 sq. km. (16.9 per cent). Pakistan has gifted 5,180 sq. km. (2.33 per cent) of the territory occupied by it in Shaksgam (Ladakh) to China.

    Pakistan has divided POK (Pakistan Occupied Kashmir) into three broad entities: i) the so-called 'AJK' (which is mainly occupied Jammu plus the Muzaffarabad area/ Kishen Ganga valley of occupied Kashmir); ii) the so-called Northern Areas (which initially consisted of 28,000 square miles in occupied Ladakh-Gilgit; India later liberated some of this land), and iii) Shaksgam. People wrongly assume that 'AJK' and POK are synonyms. 'AJK' is only one part—and a very small part, at that (5134 square miles or 13,297 square kilometres out of 86,023 square kilometres) of POK. The quotation marks around the word Azad and around the acronym AJK draw attention to the fact that 'AJK' is not an independent political entity but an occupied territory.

2   Maini, K.D., "A decision that changed the fate of Poonch," *Daily Excelsior*.

3   Mr Maini, Maj. Amin and just everyone else agrees on this figure.

4   In this case Mr. Maini's is a conservative estimate. India officially put the number of the raiders at 1,00,000. Even writers like Brian Cloughley agree that there were at least between fifteen and twenty thousand.

5   Amin, Maj (Retd) Agha Humayun, 'The war of lost opportunities', from the Internet.

6   We have seen earlier in the previous chapter as to how British officers contributed in facilitating the annexation of large chunk of territories in Gilgit-Baltistan by Pakistan, which has subsequently termed these territories as the 'Northern Areas.'

7   Ershad Mahmud, "Sardar Ibrahim remembered" *The News*, August 7, 2003.

8   Samuel Baid, "Political Crisis In POK" *Daily Excelsior*, April 1, 2004.

9   "Qayum revolts against Pakistan," *Daily Excelsior*, July 18, 1994.

10   "Pakistan Prime Minister can dismiss 'AJK' PM, says Rathore," *Khabrain*, January 27, 1995.

11   'Gang warfare in POK intensifies,' *National Herald*, October 5, 1994.

12   Were those elections really rigged? The Election Tribunal investigated the allegation and concluded that elections to seats like Muzaffarabad-Khawara had certainly been rigged. 'AJK's superior courts agreed with the Tribunal's decision.

13   Samuel Baid, "Political Crisis in POK", *Daily Excelsior*, April 1, 2004.

6

An Itinerant's Journey Through Pakistan Occupied Kashmir

Maloy Krishna Dhar

Understanding the problems of Pakistan Occupied Kashmir (POK) would require a brief journey through the pages of history between 1935 and 1947. Sheikh Abdullah and Chaudhri Ghulam Abbas of Muslim Conference had spearheaded the movement for greater devolution of power to the subjects through elected representatives. The vortex of 'One-Nation' independence movement spearheaded by the Congress and the creation of Pakistan on the basis of presumed 'Two-Nation' theory had also affected the leadership of Muslim Conference. Sheikh Abdullah charmed Nehru and Newton's 3rd Law propelled Ghulam Abbas to the lap of Jinnah. These two leaders were willing to arrive at a compromise with Sir Gopalswami Ayeangar, the then Prime Minister of Jammu and Kashmir. The two Kashmiri rivals were united on the issue of opposition to the Maharaja but disunited on most other issues. Their ego bags had no space in a common political geography. In Nehru's perception Sheikh wielded the key to Kashmir problem. Congress did not consider it necessary to tackle the Maharaja soon after 1940, when it was clear that Jinnah would not stop at anything but partition of India. He wanted his roast to be cooked according to his specifications. Pakistan had not left anything to be decided by the departing British power.

Jinnah had in his agenda the idea of merger of Junagarh with Pakistan along with chunks of Gujarat. He and other Muslim League protagonists (Nawab Salimullah of Dhaka was of Kashmiri origin) also pitched in for the Muslim majority State of J&K. The immediate tool was available in Mohammad Ibrahim who resigned from Maharaja's service and pitched in to represent Pakistan's interest. He assumed leadership of Muslim Conference and was directed by Pakistan to imitate the Congress leaders of Junagarh and set up Provisional Government at Muzaffarabad after holding meetings with Pakistan Muslim League and military officers in a Rawalpindi hotel on October 3, 1947. Ibrahim was set up as 'Prime Minister' with Ghulam Nabi Gilkar as the 'President.' From this nucleus Pakistan built upon agitations in Poonch, Mirpur, Kotli and nearby areas and later pushed in the armed tribals and regular army. POK was born in Pakistani mind on Muzaffarabad territory long before Pakistan militarily intervened. The rest is history.

Since then historical accounts, scholastic dissertations, diplomatic ambivalence and strategic sabre rattling have dominated the public and geopolitical domains in India, Pakistan and the international community on the 'disputed flashpoint' of Kashmir. It's not my intention to throw another pedantic brickbat at the readers. They are already confused and have ceased to think beyond the Vale of Kashmir, falls, Chinars, shikara rides and daily body bags. In Indian political mind and in the cranial cavity of several intellectuals and Track II diplomats Indo-Pak dispute is limited to the Vale of Kashmir, Ladakh, Jammu and a strip of land described by Pakistan as 'Azad Kashmir'.

Indian political class, some specialists and genealogical bureaucrats and major media mughals have also started projecting Kashmir problem pertaining to the areas mentioned above. Indian mind is being prepared to link the Kashmir problem for another partition along the LoC. Muzaffarabad, Kotli and Mirpur are distant dreams.

Pakistan Occupied Kashmir comprises the Muzaffarabad region, adjacent to Islamabad, Rawalpindi, Murree, Manshera and Gujarat etc., strategic border areas of Pakistan. By grabbing these areas in 1948 Pakistan acquired a strategic depth against India's conventional war thrusts. By technically integrating the POK areas with its main territory Pakistan has flagrantly violated the UN resolutions, Tashkent and Simla Agreements. Pundits have elaborated these aspects of Pakistan's perfidious activities.

Indian mind is not trained to think in terms of understanding that vast areas of the kingdom of Kashmir, besides the Muzaffarabad region described by Pakistan as Azad Kashmir, are under Pakistani and Chinese occupation. These territories of the kingdom of Kashmir, which merged into India, have almost disappeared from Indian memory and are considered 'technical cartographic definition'.

My journey is limited to trekking along the occupied territories of Kashmir and remind Indians, through a pedestrian's approach, the need for renewal of Indian interest in the area, which is vitally important to our future strategic planning.

China had grabbed the Aksai Chin region taking advantage of lack of military planning and preparedness and absence of a deep geostrategic understanding of the Chinese designs. Though shown as a 'disputed area' in cartographic terms, China has virtually integrated Aksai Chin with Tibet Autonomous Region. China had also cajoled Pakistan to cede 1/3rd of Jammu & Kashmir's Northern Area (Gilgit-Baltistan) in the vital Karakoram Pass areas in 1963.

India did very little diplomatically and through friendly world powers and the UN to prevent Pakistan from ceding a territory of Jammu and Kashmir, which had legally merged with India. Validity of the 1963 Sino-Pak accord is questionable under international law as at the time of signing of the accord

Pakistan was only having actual control on defence of the area ceded. Text of the Sino-Pak Agreement violates all international norms and resolutions imposed by the UNO on India and Pakistan over the 'Kashmir dispute'.

"The Government of the People's Republic of China and the Government of Pakistan, having agreed, with a view to ensuring the prevailing peace and tranquillity on the border, to formally delimit and demarcate the boundary between China's Sinking and the contiguous areas the defence of which is under the actual control of Pakistan in a spirit of fairness, reasonableness, mutual understanding and mutual accommodation, and on the basis of the ten principles as enunciated in the Bandung Conference.

Being convinced that this would not only give full expression to the desire of the people of China and Pakistan for the development of good neighbourly and friendly relations, but also help safeguard Asian and world peace.

Have resolved for this purpose to conclude the present agreement and have appointed as their respective plenipotentiaries the following. For the Government of the People's Republic of China, Chen Yi, Minister of Foreign Affairs. For the Government of the Pakistan, Zulfikar Bhutto, Minister of External Affairs.

Who, having mutually examined their full powers and found them to be in good and due form have agreed" on the delimitation.

The political class and the governments in India have so far not made average Indians aware of the fact that Pakistan has ceded $1/3^{rd}$ of J&K to China on the strength of assumed parameter 'the defence of which (*the ceded area*) is under the actual control of Pakistan'. What follows from this assumption? Pakistan reserves the right to cede the Gilgit and Baltistan areas of J&K to China or America on some other strategic consideration on the same plea of *de facto* military presence in the area. It is as bad in international law as is the forcible amalgamation of parts of Gaza strip, Western Bank and Golan Heights by Israel. While Pakistan joins voice with other Arab governments to condemn Israel, it has no explanation to give to the people of J&K and India; the legal inheritor of the territories of the Maharaja of J&K. India has also not kept the item on diplomatic dinner plates in Agra, Delhi and Islamabad.

A detailed reading of the land mass transferred to China in 1963 indicates that Pakistan was preparing the grounds for a decisive round of war against India in 1965 with tacit Chinese help and silent nod from America, which was using Pakistan to build a bridge with China. After the devastating defeat in 1962 a stupefied India could do very little to stop China from grabbing a territory through deceit. Article 2 of the treaty delineates the ceded area, which include important Passes like Mintake Daban, Parpik, Yutr Daban, Muztagh, and Karakoram.

The perfidious action was given a legal cover by the insertion of Article 6, which reads as follows:

Article 6. "The two parties have agreed that after the settlement of the Kashmir dispute between Pakistan and India, the sovereign authority concerned will reopen negotiations with the Government of the People's Republic of China on the boundary as described in Article Two of the present agreement, so as to sign a formal boundary treaty to replace the present agreement, provided that in the event of the sovereign authority being Pakistan, the provisions of the present agreement and of the aforesaid protocol shall be maintained in the formal boundary treaty to be signed between the People's Republic of China and Pakistan."

This means Pakistan ceded certain important passes which were historically considered strategically important to ensure Indian security and interests in certain areas of China and adjacent USSR (now Central Asian Republics). It also means that India has to reopen negotiation either with China or Pakistan depending on the 'final settlement of Kashmir dispute'.

Indian people are in the dark about this sordid international transaction between China and Pakistan, done under the very noses of the Cold War Allied Powers and the UN. In 1963, Nehru government was not in a position to adopt a military stand on this vital issue. Its diplomatic efforts were also muted and merely formal. In 2006 India should be in a position to reclaim the entire Kashmir from Pakistan including areas occupied by China in Aksai Chin and Karakoram tracts in Hunza region. This strip of land is geo-strategically very important for India.

The strangest oddity of the situation is that some pro-Pakistani political fronts in Jammu & Kashmir vociferously resent any talk of dilution of Article 370 and closer ties with the Union. They, however, remain criminally silent when Pakistan gifts a chunk of Kashmir territory to China.

The story of annexation of the Gilgit Agency and Baltistan (Skardu) is equally indicative of Indian failure to react fast to illegal geographical realignment of the historically sovereign territory of the Maharaja of Kashmir. Some neat tricks, and suspected Pak-British collaboration achieved more than what Pakistan achieved in the war of 1948 and from subsequent political and diplomatic paralysis of the government of India.

Pakistan repeated the show it staged by stoking rebellion in Poonch, Mirpur and Kotli. It started negotiating with the figurehead rulers of the area and the *Sardars*. Mostly Muslims, the Gilgit Scouts were also influenced by Pakistan through local religious leaders, *Sardars* and potentates. Like the 'Provisional Government of POK' a move was mooted by Shah Rais Khan to set up 'The Gilgit Republic'. History bears evidence of Pakistani connectivity of Rais Khan.

Lord Mountbatten was in constant touch with London, Nehru and Jinnah on the future of Kashmir. His special concern over Gilgit was brought up in his letter to Listowel, Secretary of State:

"NEW DELHI, 29 April 1947, 11.50 pm Received: 29 April, 11.40 pm... .

1. No. 941-P. Gilgit subdivision is at present administered by H.E. the Crown Representative under 60 years agreement made with Kashmir Government in 1935.

2. Passes to Gilgit are only open during the summer months and Political Department, therefore, proposes that the agreement should be terminated during September 1947 thus enabling *the Crown Representative's establishment which includes two Political officers to be removed before termination of paramountcy and giving Kashmir Government opportunity to make suitable alternative arrangements for administration of the area.*

3. Department of External Affairs and Defence Departments confirm that premature termination of agreement as proposed will not prejudice All India interests in the sphere of foreign relations and defence. But Nehru has suggested that the question of terminating the agreement be reconsidered next Spring (*sic*) when nature of Kashmir's relationship to the Union of India will be much clearer. *(Nehru had bargained for time.)*

4. I have given this suggestion careful consideration but do not think it can be accepted for the following reasons. Firstly, suggestion directly conflicts with the *accepted policy of achieving greatest possible devolution of paramountcy by the end of 1947.* Secondly, if decision is deferred till Spring 1948 it will be impossible, for practical reasons, to give effect to it by June 1948. Thirdly, administratively it will be immensely difficult and complex task to complete final transfer of power throughout India by June 1948 and I cannot think it prudent to complicate the task still further by postponing decisions, which can be made now without prejudice to interests of any party. Fourthly, postponement would be strongly resented by Kashmir and interpreted as breach of faith.

5. Subject to your approval I propose, therefore, to terminate the agreement not later than October 1st 1947. Very early reply is requested as the Resident Kashmir should be informed of decision by the end of April.

6. This is a case which falls to be dealt with under final sentence of paragraph 12 of Prime Minister's statement of February 20th and I propose merely to inform Nehru personally of decision."

London was in a hurry to escape from India. Listowel replied by telegram on May 8, 1947: "I agree with the line you take and I approve the proposal contained in your para 5. With reference to your para 6, I understand Nehru has now accepted your decision."

Indian records are silent on Nehru's 'agreement' to Mounbatten's proposal. Did Nehru request for some temporary 'military buffer' for Gilgit-Baltistan and the whole of Kashmir, taking into consideration Maharaja's inability to defend his territory? No one has the answer. Military leaders of the day are eloquently silent about this.

After June 3, the Political Department returned the area to the Maharaja and the Gilgit Scouts were also handed over to him. Major William Brown, a soldier of Scottish origin, was in command of the Gilgit Scouts. Brown's Commission was transferred from King George VI to the Maharaja of Jammu & Kashmir. The king was in the process of establishing his authority in the area after abrupt withdrawal by the British. London had not heeded to Indian suggestion to phased withdrawal after the political future of J&K was finally decided.

William Brown in his memoir *The Gilgit Rebellion* mentions that, taking advantage of the withdrawal of the British, the Pakistani authorities incited the Muslim tribesmen and arranged their congregation in Gilgit town. They were incited to kill Hindu and Sikh officials and other J&K citizen. Absence of authority, especially inability and helplessness of the circumstances of India, allured Pakistan to incite Poonch, Mirpur type rebellion under leaders like Rais Khan.

Major Brown was the only military authority in Gilgit and his colleague Captain Mathieson was in Chilas. Major Brown came under severe pressure from his superior Col. Bacon at

Peshawar and Col. Iskander Mirza, Defence Secretary of Pakistan to declare merger of Gilgit Agency with Pakistan. On the morning of November 4, 1947 he raised Pakistani flag over his headquarters.

Representatives of Pakistan government waited for the rulers at their *qillas* when the Hunza and Nagar rulers were enjoying Maharaja's hospitality in Srinagar. Events in Gilgit overtook the Maharaja and the rulers of Hunza and Nagar responded positively to overtures from Pakistan, when they realised that the Maharaja had no physical means to assert his sovereignty.

After two weeks, the Government of Pakistan sent an administrator to take over civil power in the region, during which Brown effectively exercised it. Questions were asked in London but they were not unhappy with the turn of events. Neither Lord Mountbatten nor Listowel had any answer to these conspiracies hatched between junior British officers and the Pakistani leaders. Nehru had no vision of Kashmir beyond Sheikh Abdullah. His tunnel vision was further opalesced by Mounbatten's indifferent shrug.

The details of Pakistan's deceit and treachery in respect of the territory of J&K may take volumes to recount. Some brief details have been narrated to prepare a canvas for projecting the present state of affairs in Pakistan Occupied Kashmir including Gilgit-Baltistan a tract of land and people who have very little in common with Pakistan except that they profess different shades of Islam.

Pakistan has blatantly segregated Gilgit-Baltistan from the so-called 'Azad Kashmir.' The latter was granted a sham constitution and election process. For all practical purposes, the 'AJK' is ruled by Islamabad through certain dummies controlled by the army and the ISI. We will comment on these aspects in later paragraphs.

As we journey through Gilgit-Baltistan the 'Northern Areas' we come across a different kaleidoscope. The area is divided into five administrative units: Gilgit, Baltistan, Diamir, Ghizer and Ghanche. A population of nearly 2 million inhabits the 72,495 square kilometer geographical spread. The main ethnic groups are Baltis (Balawaris), Yashkuns, Mughals, Kashmiris, Pathans, Ladakhis, Tajik, Uzbek, Mongol, Turkmen and population of Greek origin. Though Pakistan is trying to impose Urdu in the Gilgit and Baltistan the main languages spoken are, Balti, Shina, Brushaski, Khawer, Wakhi, Turki, Tibeti, and Pushto.

Religious sect-wise breakdown of population in the Gilgit-Baltistan is:

Gilgit – 60% Shia, 40% Sunni (imported from Pakistan); Nagar—100% Shia, Hunza, Yasin, Punial, Ishkoman, Gupis—100% Ismaili (Aghakhani), Chilas, Darel, 100% Sunni, Astor—90% Sunni and 10% Shia and Baltistan—98% Shia and 2% Sunni. There are about 10% Nurbakshis in the region. The Sunnis are predominantly Hanafi with sprinkles of Maliki and Hanbali sects.

Present political status of the Gilgit-Baltistan is different from the one granted to 'AJK'. The areas defined as 'AJK' have been granted the luxury of multi-party democratically elected government with a Governor and Prime Minister, all controlled by Islamabad through the Minister in charge of Kashmir affairs, the military and the Inter Services Intelligence. The Gilgit and Baltistan have been denied even that modicum of democracy. It is administratively not a part of 'AJK'. Pakistan Supreme Court has recognised that the area is also not a part of Pakistan. However, Islamabad rules directly under the Frontier Crime Regulation framed by the British. The Minister of State for Kashmir and Northern Areas (KANA) runs the administration with the help of six outside officers and an elected council, which is manipulated by the army and the ISI. The Minister for KANA exercises all political, economic and administrative powers. Recently the Gilgit and Baltistan Legislative Council (NALC) had passed a resolution to abolish

KANA's control. The members were banned entry to all government offices by the Pakistani Minister.

Having described the instruments used by Pakistan to annex a vast area of J&K, it is necessary to highlight the abuses and injustice heaped on the people of AJK and Gilgit-Baltistan.

Gilgit-Baltistan occupied by Pakistan is seething with discontent. Planned induction of Punjabis, Pathans, and other sub-nationalities to the region has started altering the population pattern. The Sunni militant organisations are being encouraged to set up separate mosques and madrasas. Instances of desecration of places of worship of other sects are not uncommon. The ISI has planted the seeds of sectarian violence in Gilgit-Baltistan.

Pakistan is notoriously divided on sectarian lines, basically the Shia-Sunni tussles. The Shia and Sunni forces are organised on militant lines and this tussle from Pakistan has also shifted to Gilgit-Baltistan. The predominant Shia, Ismaili and Nurbakshi communities in the region have come under planned attacks from the Sunnis. In recent months there have been serious clashes leading to considerable loss of lives and properties.

Quoted by the daily *Insaf* (January 7, 2005) leader of Jamaat-ud-Dawa (former Laskar-e-Toiba) Hafiz Saeed claimed that the Gilgit and Baltistan of Pakistan were being turned apostate (*murtad*) through the Aga Khan Foundation. He said Pakistan was not Islamic; therefore, each Muslim should enforce Shariat in his house. According to him Hindus, Jews and Christians were active in the garb of NGOs and were being protected by them. Hafiz Saeed is known for strong sectarian views. It is obvious that he was building up the mythical case of an Ismaili conspiracy in Gilgit-Baltistan. The word *murtad* is significant because the punishment for a *murtad* is death in the eyes of the Islamists. It is clear that some vigilant groups are regularly punishing the Ismailis and Shias. Unfortunately, the military administration has not yet woken up to the emerging fissures in the region. They encourage it, because the processes strengthen Pakistan's presence in the area.

Besides religious strife political tremor is also shaking the 'AJK' and Gilgit-Baltistan. The people of so-called 'Azad Kashmir' have started resenting and voicing protests against Punjabi domination and recent developments indicate that the people of 'AJK' are restless over demands of better political and economic status. They are exasperated with the activities of Islamist jiahdis, most of whom are from Punjab and who carry out ISI designed proxy war inside Kashmir valley. Of the approximate total strength of jihadists trained in 'AJK' only five per cent belong to 'AJK'.

Administratively 'AJK' is divided into five major units: Muzzaffarabad, Bagh, Rawalkot, Kotli and Mirpur. Though most of the population is Sunni, the 'AJK' people are more organised on lines of *biradari*, like the Abbasi, Sudhan and Sithan etc. At present Islamabad is placing considerable trust on the Sudhan *biradari* at the consternation of the Abbasis and Sithans etc. This would be commented briefly in later paragraphs.

Political rumblings in the 'AJK' have not started with the recently held rigged election. Way back in 1990-91, when Pakistan was planning escalated violent proxy-war in J&K, the political leaders of 'AJK' had started voicing demand for 'independence'. In 1991 Islamabad dismissed, "Prime Minister", of 'AJK'. Mumtaz Rathore for insubordination and demanding better rights for the people. He was arrested and flown to a Pakistani prison. In the 1996 elections political leaders supporting 'independence' were barred. Parties and candidates, who wished to participate on the platform of independence and refused to sign the declaration calling accession of 'AJK' to Pakistan an article of faith, were denied the right to field candidates. The willing political leaders were forced to sign the declaration calling accession of 'AJK' to Pakistan as an article of faith. The President, PM, Minister, Speaker, MLA and MLC of 'AJK' have to take an oath: *"that*

I will remain loyal to the country (Pakistan) *and the cause of accession of the state of Jammu and Kashmir to Pakistan".*
However, such oaths militate against UN resolutions. Pakistan cannot make such demand of the people of 'AJK'. The people of 'AJK' are given no rights in Pakistan. Neither they can vote in Pakistan's general elections, nor take their grievances to the Pakistani Supreme Court. They cannot hold any public office in Pakistan. Pakistan National Budget makes no provision for the region.

Old horse of 'AJK', "President" Sikander Hayat Khan, was removed through a voice vote in the Assembly in 1996 after he demanded share of Pakistan's budget, better self-rule provisions and minimization of interference by the army and the ISI. Similarly, Shaukat Ali Kashmiri, chairperson of the United Kashmir People's National Party (UKPNP) based in 'AJK', was arrested by the ISI for voicing dissent. After his release, Shaukat Ali Kashmiri condemned the killing of innocent villagers by the Pakistan-backed terrorists. In fact, he tried to draw attention of the world community to the facts of torture on local men and women (sexual abuse included) by the jihadi groups like the LeT, JeM and HuM. He was later hunted out and is now sheltered in Switzerland. Justice (Retd) Mohd Akram, President of the J&K Human Rights Movement has listed specific human rights violations by Pakistan intelligence agencies and 'AJK' police. Akram's movement in 'AJK' has been restricted.

Most opposition political parties have condemned 'AJK' elections of July 2006. The elections were held for the 49-seat Assembly. Only 29 constituencies were allotted to the eight Districts of POK, 12 seats were earmarked for Jammu and Kashmir 'refugees' living in various parts of Pakistan (mohajir voters). Eight seats were reserved for women and one each for the religious scholars, technocrats and overseas Kashmiris.

A total of 369 candidates from 17 political parties and independents contested the polls. In the results declared on July 13, the ruling AJK Muslim Conference won 20 seats, the PML 4, the PPP 7, Jammu Kashmir Peoples' Party 1, the Muttahida Quami Movement (MQM) 2, and independents 6. Voting for the 12 mohajir seats was held in Pakistan, not in 'AJK' areas. The military-ISI establishment manipulates these seats to maintain Islamabad's stranglehold on the regime in Muzaffarabad. Various opposition leaders including those of 'AJK' Muslim Conference, People's Muslim League and All Parties National Alliance have condemned the rigged election.

To top it Islamabad managed to get the resignation of Major Gen Mohammad Anwar Khan, belonging to the powerful Sudhan tribe of Tain village in Poonch and got him elected as the 'AJK President.' The 'AJK' Muslim Conference was forced to accept Anwar as the official nominee of the party. Anwar Khan is related to Lt Gen Mohammed Aziz, former Vice Chief of the General Staff, in the GHQ. He was Deputy Director General of the ISI under Lt Gen Aziz. He was responsible for directing and mobilizing the Al Qaeda, Harkat-ul-Mujahideen (HuM), the Lashkar-e-Toiba (LeT), Al Badr and Jaish-e-Mohammad (JeM) cadres. With Gen. Anwar ensconced in Muzaffrabad it is anticipated that the ISI will escalate Pakistani offensive in Indian J&K and inside the rest of India.

Before we serve the hot dog of jihadi activities of Pakistan from 'AJK' we may like to taste the salad of prevailing political discontent in Gilgit-Baltistan. Shorn of any development activity and devolution of power the people of Gilgit-Baltistan are sharply reacting to the hegemonist attitude of Islamabad.

Pakistan maintains, besides the Northern Light Infantry formations and detachments of Regular Army some seasonal tanzeem camps at Marol, Baghicha, Dou, Dhappa, a place between the basins of Khepchan Brok and Satpura and Skardu areas of Baltistan and Bunji, Damiyor, Gilgit and Hamuchal in Gilgit region. These are supervised by the Northern Light Infantry (NLI) and the Inter Services Intelligence (ISI). The ISI has started recruiting jihadis from amongst the Baltis and Gilgitis with a view to broaden their Islamist horizon.

The local protagonists cite several instances of persecution by the KANA authorities. A local Superintendent of Police lost his job because his wife, a member of NALC criticized Pakistan for her husband's suspension. Mr. Saif Rehman member NALC was jailed on treason charges simply because he admonished a Pakistani employee. Later ISI sponsored terrorists killed Rehman when he tried to intervene in a sectarian feud. It is reported that more than 100 political leaders and workers have been charged with sedition and have been severely tortured before dumping them in Pakistani jails.

According to Abdul Hamid Khan of "Balawaristan National Front"—an organisation which propagates independence for the region, on October 11, 2005, some Al-Qaida terrorists opened fired on Shia Muslims in Basen, 58 kilometer from Gilgit, and killed two. One injured terrorist was arrested by the local police. He was forcibly taken away by the Pakistani Rangers. Local people protested against the act of rescue of the Al Qaeda terrorist. To drive in terror the ISI kidnapped a Shia youth and killed him. While his relatives and colleagues protested on October 13, 2005 Pakistani Rangers opened fire and killed seven people including the former chairman of Gilgit Municipal Committee. According to the Pakistani newspaper *Dawn*, dated October 15, 2005, the death toll in firing in Gilgit mounted to 12 after six more bodies, including that of a woman, were found in different areas of the city.

According to reports from Gilgit the ISI had kidnapped a Shia teacher, Mr. Bilal Hussain from Jamal Hotel Gilgit City on September 10, 2005. He was taken to Islamabad for interrogation. He is now presumed dead. The Balawaris allege that Brigadier Riaz-ullah Khan Chib, ISI in-charge of Joint Intelligence Bureau, which deals with internal security matters, 'AJK' and Gilgit-Baltistan and his station commander in Gilgit-Baltistan, Colonel Fahim had adopted a planned policy to suppress all Shia, Ismaili and Nurbakshi agitations demanding better political status. To achieve this objective the ISI had inducted Punjabi and Pathan employees in the area. Several killings and kidnappings have been reported since 2003. Many details of atrocities by the ISI agents, Jihadi tanzeems and Sunni sectarians have been reported. These are not unknown to the world community.

Amir Humza Qureshi, founder of the Gilgit-Baltistan Jamhoori Mahaz, has also highlighted issues pertaining to Human Rights violations and cruelty perpetrated on the people of Gilgit-Baltistan. In his opinion, the people of Gilgit-Baltistan faced more human rights violations than Pakistan published 'repression' on people in 'Indian Held Kashmir'.

A few words must be added about the Northern Light Infantry (NLI). The NLI was created in 1973 after merging the Gilgit Scouts, Northern Scouts and Karakoram Scouts. The NLI played a crucial role during Pakistani aggression in Kargil sector in 1999. Its ranks suffered serious casualties. However, Pakistani media publicised heroic roles played by the jihadi tanzeems. The people of Gilgit and Baltistan region resented this. To ward off a revolt Pakistan conferred on the NLI the status of a regular regiment only after the Kargil war. There are accusations that the Balawaristani protagonists are trying to subvert the NLI. To prevent such possibilities Islamabad has attached special ISI units under the garb of the MI field units to each NLI Company. According to sources inside Balawaristan movement, Pakistan has started gradually inducting Punjabi and Pathan elements in the NLI. However, this is yet to stir up the well-trained and motivated NLI personnel drawn from Gilgit-Baltistan.

Indian Public mind is by and large aware of existence of ISI managed Jihadi training camps in 'AJK'. With Major Gen (Retd) Mohammad Anwar Khan at the helm of affairs in Muzaffarabad 'AJK' watchers comment that it has become truly an ISI territory. Pakistan has extensively used the 'AJK' territory to house, train and motivate the J&K militant groups like the redundant JKLF. Since 1988-89, coinciding with Pakistan's Afghan sojourn and tryst with the Sikh terrorists in Punjab, Islamabad branched out to the 'AJK' through ISI covert operations to set up camps for the jihadi groups and malcontent elements from Indian Kashmir. Before Brigadier Abdullah (2003-4) the operations were supervised by the Muzaffarabad station chief Col Shauqat Chima. Camps for the Harkat-ul-Ansar (Harkat-ul-Mujahideen) and other tanzeems were established under cover of regular army camps. Infiltration routes were surveyed and compatible groups were generated in Kashmir valley. The operational thrusts gathered momentum after Benazir Bhutto assumed power.

Initially training camps for Pakistani jihadis and Kashmiri youths were set up at Muzaffarabad, Bagh, Kotli, New Mirpur, Tain, Kahuta (POK), Rawalkot, Rajdhani Baratla, Bhimber, Panjgiran, Domal and Khairgam. Later, as the operations escalated more camps were set up and integrated with camps in Punjab and NWFP. Soon after the year end earthquake in 2005 Indian agencies declared that tanzeems like Lashkar-e-Toiba (LeT), Jaish-e-Mohammed (JeM), Al-Badr and Tehrik-e-Mujahideen and Hizbul Mujahideen lost about 15,000 jihadis. Claims were also made that camps at Rawalkot, Manshera, Nikial, Kotli, Bagh, Palandri, Dudhnial, Deolian, Kalighati and, of course, Muzaffarabad, were destroyed by the quake. However, the United Jihad Council rebutted these claims.

According to latest reports emanating from Indian agencies the ISI used services of Pakistani diplomats of Waziri origin and Waziri Army officers to negotiate with the Waziri Sirdars for getting their respective areas vacated by Al Qaeda. ISI reportedly paid heavily to some of the *Sardars*, namely of Dwa Toi, Ali Khel, Zira Khel (South Waziristan) and Mardana, Maduri Bangash, Sangroba (North Waziristan) etc. They have persuaded the *Sardars* to allow the Qaeda groups to move out from their respective pockets. These Qaeda fighters are of Waziri, Afghan, Uzbek, Arabs and Pakistani (Punjabi) origin.

About 70 Al Qaeda men have been brought by ISI to Baglakot, Naukot (NWFP) camps and Samgam glacier camp, Rajdhani, Rawalkot and Salian camps in 'AJK'. Major Sabur Usman of ISI is reportedly handling the jihadis and Al Qaeda elements. He liases with the Lashkar, Jaish and HuM cadres and supervises their training, infiltration and action plan.

The jihadi tanzeems had taken up intensive relief work amongst the quake affected people taking advantage of laxity of the administration and Army's preoccupation with own losses and jaundiced perception that India might launch pre-emptive attack taking opportunity of the natural disaster. Lashkar-e-Toiba, renamed Jamat-ud-Dawa and other groups worked side by side with the foreign relief agencies. Pakistan's allowance to the jihadi tanzeems to work at the grass roots level has strengthened their hold on the populace. In fact, the ISI and the jihadi tanzeems rule the 'AJK' territory. The so-called elected government is a window dressing.

In his book *Last Colony of the Twenty First Century* Abdul Hamid Khan of BNF asserted, "Pakistani terrorists, drug and arms smugglers, Taliban and other terrorists are speedily settled in Balawaristan to turn the indigenous people into a minority." According to him the terrorists were also used by the ISI for "hostile activities" against Jammu and Kashmir, Afghanistan's Northern Alliance, Central Asian countries, Russia and the Muslim-dominated Sinkiang province in China. He has alleged that the ISI works in close cooperation with the Jamat-e-Islami to recruit youths for training at terrorist training camps in Gilgit-Baltistan region and Mansehra district, adjacent to Jammu and Kashmir.

Khan asserted that youths from Pakistan, Afghanistan and Kashmir are trained at camps run by the ISI in Ghowadi Skardu, Darel, Yashote, Astore and Gilgit. The youths are "instigated against non-Muslims of Afghanistan, Kashmir, Chechnya, the US and other countries. Abdul Hamid Khan is an insider. We have no reason to doubt in his assertions.

Pakistan has used both 'AJK' and Gilgit-Baltistan against Indian interests. In fact, Pakistani military build up in the areas has been augmented after 1999 Kargil war. Elaborate roads, airstrips and helipads have been constructed within three kilometres of the LoC. Besides the High Altitude Training Centre near Gilgit, Pakistan Army has set up jointly with the SSG a guerrilla commando training centre near Skardu. Existing airfields have been improved to accommodate sophisticated fighter-bombers. Military encirclement of India from these areas has reached a level of sophistication. Pakistan has maintained these areas of Kashmir at minimal cost and has been carrying out a low cost war against India from these bases. Is there anybody in India to consider how could the country respond to military encirclement of India from these areas and how could Pakistan's cost-ratio be escalated? Is there anybody to listen what the people of the so called 'AJK' and Gilgit-Baltistan have to say about Pakistani occupation?

7

Suppression of Gilgit-Baltistan

Samuel Baid

A Washington datelined story reported by Pakistan's *Daily Times* on February 27, 2006, said Pakistani embassies abroad were distributing a booklet containing a map of Jammu and Kashmir but showing Gilgit-Baltistan (or Northern Areas as Pakistanis call it) as a separate territory. The whole Jammu and Kashmir is shown as a single State without the dividing Line of Control or line of ceasefire. The newspaper recalls the 1994 verdict of Pakistan Occupied Kashmir's Supreme Court which said Northern Areas were part of the State of Jammu and Kashmir as it was in 1947.

During the last about 60 years Pakistan's stand on Gilgit-Baltistan has been very unsteady. Its leaders have made their people believe that this region belongs to Pakistan. But in its own courts as well as in the courts of Pakistan Occupied Kashmir (POK) or Azad Jammu and Kashmir 'AJK', Pakistan has taken the stand that it is not possible to give the people of Gilgit-Baltistan any constitutional rights because these areas do not belong to it. In the Atlas of Pakistan published by the Surveyor General of Pakistan in 1986, territory of Gilgit-Baltistan is left undefined while the rest of Jammu and Kashmir is stamped "Disputed".

But Pakistan has always acted as an untitled owner of this territory. In March 1963, Pakistan gave away 2700 sq miles from Hunza to China. Mir of Hunza protested but to no avail. In 1974 Hunza was merged with 'Northern Areas' by the then Prime Minister of Pakistan, Mr. Zulfikar Ali Bhutto. It is said Mr. Bhutto was annoyed with the Mir of Hunza for his protest against ceding part of his territory to China.

General Pervez Musharraf's announcement on January 17, 2006, that Pakistan's dam building plan would start with the construction of Bhasha dam shocked the people of Gilgit-Baltistan. This decision was announced in a typical authoritarian way that marks Pak Establishment's attitude to Gilgit-Baltistan and even to Balochistan. By this attitude, the Establishment wanted to emphasise that the people of Gilgit-Baltistan were not the owners of their land and its natural resources. More on Bhasha later.

In POK nobody can fight the Assembly elections unless he/she swears by accession of Kashmir to Pakistan. For the elections to the Northern Areas Legislative Council (NALC) there is no such bar. Also, only Pakistan-based political parties take part in the elections to NALC. The POK-based parties like the Muslim Conference do not, or more correctly are not allowed to take part in the NALC elections. The objective in this pattern is very clear: Pakistan wants to project Gilgit-Baltistan as an "undisputed" separate entity which is out of the purview of United Nations Resolutions on Kashmir.

The purpose of this paper is to study Gilgist-Baltistan which for the past 60 years has existed as Pakistan's serfdom. Strangely the plight of the people of Gilgit-Baltistan has not provoked the conscience of world human rights organisations. Here the local people have no rights. Pakistan refuses to give them any civil rights on the plea that it is not its territory.

Gilgit-Baltistan is spread over 28,000 sq miles and its population is about 20 lakh — mainly Shias. The British rulers of India followed a policy of keeping Gilgit-Baltistan isolated from the rest of the State of Kashmir and for using this sensitive region to keep a watch on the activities of Russia. Gilgit-Baltistan does not border Russia but it overlooks that country. It (Gilgit-Baltistan), however, touches China and Afghanistan. In 1877 the British set up Gilgit Agency and appointed an Agent who acted as the ruler of this territory. In 1935 the British rulers took Gilgit-Baltistan on a 60-year lease from Maharaja Hari Singh but decided to return it to him in 1947 when the British paramountcy came to an end. However, as many historians have noted, the British officers of Gilgit Scouts provoked a revolt against the return of this territory back to Hari Singh. The Gilgit Scouts revolted and set up "People's Republic of Baltistan and Gilgit" on November 1, 1947. But this Republic existed only for about two weeks. On April 28, 1949, Muslim Conference leaders Mohammad Ibrahim and Ghulam Abbas, who were then the "President" of POK and President of the Muslim Conference, respectively, signed an agreement with Pakistan's Minister without portfolio M.A. Gurmani surrendering the administration of Gilgit-Baltistan to the Government of Pakistan.

After six decades, the people of Gilgit-Baltistan are realising that Muslim Conference had no business to sign such an agreement. However, the present stand of the Government of Pakistan is that such an agreement never existed. After taking over the administration of Gilgit-Baltistan, the Pakistani Government restored the black law called Frontier Crimes Regulations (FCR). The FCR treated the people of Gilgit-Baltistan as brute criminals. The Pakistan government made it clear to the people of Gilgit-Baltistan that they would continue to be ruled as during the British rule.

Pakistan also restored the British ban on political activities in Gilgit-Baltistan. The Muslim Conference (MC) which had opened its local branch was ordered to wind it up fast. Till today the MC obeys this order, even though Pakistan-based political parties have been allowed to take part in the NALC elections. Incidentally, the name Northern Areas Legislative

Council does not mean that the elected members can legislate. 'Legislative' has been inserted to fool the world.

When Pakistan took over the administration of Gilgit-Baltistan, it put it under an agent from North West Frontier Province (NWFP) armed with the revived FCR. Care was taken to ensure that no interaction took place between the people of Gilgit-Baltistan and "Azad" Kashmir.

If a crude simile is allowed here, Pakistan's relationship with Gilgit-Baltistan is like that of a man and his helpless keep who is exploited but has no legal rights. Pakistan has treated itself as a lawful owner of this territory without giving it rights and an identity. Pakistan extends its taxes to it; flies its own flag on official buildings; makes school children sing its national anthem and consider its heroes as their own.

The so-called Northern Areas Legislative Council (NALC) is a big hoax. It has no speaker, no leader of the opposition and, above all, it has no powers to legislate. All rules for this territory are made by Pakistan's Minister for Kashmir and Northern Areas Affairs who is not an elected member of the NALC but is the Chief Executive of this territory. The Deputy Chief Executive is an elected local man and is based in Gilgit. But for all practical purposes he is a powerless entity.

The successive Pakistani Governments have given an impression of doing reforms in the administrative set-up but they were no more than old wine in new bottles. For example, the first change in the administrative set-up was made in 1950, where the control of Gilgit-Baltistan was transferred to Pakistan's Ministry of Kashmir Affairs. Thus, the real control of this territory passed on to the Pakistani bureaucrats. And despite about half a dozen reforms since then, this continues to be the real administrative pattern.

In September 1974, the then Prime Minster Zulfikar Ali Bhutto disbanded Gilgit Scouts and abolished FCR. That paved the way for political activities in Gilgit-Baltistan. He merged Hunza with rest of Gilgit-Baltistan. The Mir of Hunza,

Mohammad Jamal, was arrested when he protested. India protested at this merger.

Mr. Bhutto was making these changes as if he was dealing with one of Pakistan's provinces. His reforms did not solve any of the problems the people were facing. Hence there were agitations. Later when Gen Zia ul Haq overthrew Mr. Bhutto's government in July 1977, he put Gilgit-Baltistan under martial law, as he had done in Pakistan. When he set up his Majlis-i-Shoora in 1981 he nominated three persons from Gilgit-Baltistan as observers on it. This was Gen Zia's attempt to placate those who wanted Gilgit-Baltistan to be made Pakistan's fifth province or merge it with NWFP. There were two other suggestions, or rather demands: merge Gilgit-Baltistan with "Azad" Kashmir or give it the status which "Azad" Kashmir enjoys, i.e., its own separate constitution and a State Assembly.

Gen Zia was not able to accept any of those demands. He is accused by the Pakistan's press of trying to kill the local demands by creating a sectarian rift. Shias and Islamails form the majority of the 20-lakh strong population of Gilgit-Baltistan. Gen Zia is accused of engineering the May 1988 Shia-Sunni riots. Thousands of armed Sunni tribesmen descended from Pakistan and butchered Shias. "Nobody stopped them. They destroyed crops and houses, lynched and burnt people to death in the villages around Gilgit town. The number of dead and injured was put in the hundreds. But numbers alone talk nothing of the savagery of the invading hordes and the chilling impact it has left on these peaceful valley."[1] A repeat of this carnage occurred in 1992 when Sunnis from Chitral and Kohistan (both in NWFP) invaded Gilgit.[2] The military intervened as late as after eight days. This gave local Shias the reason to keep themselves militarily prepared to meet the Sunni onslaughts.

Whenever the people of Gilgit-Baltistan demanded civil and constitutional rights the answer was bloody sectarian riots.

Moen Qureshi, who worked as Pakistan's caretaker Prime Minister between July and October 1993 announced certain reforms just on the eve of relinquishing his office. He expanded the strength of Northern Areas Council to 26 and made the Chief Executive its Chairman.

Ms. Benazir Bhutto, who came after Mr. Qureshi, gave financial and administrative powers to the Chief Executive. She created the post of a Deputy Chief Executive who was elected and was based in Gilgit. Ms. Bhutto's reforms gave the Northern Areas Council legislative, financial and executive powers only on paper.

Ms. Bhutto's reforms did not really do anything to answer the demands of the people of Gilgit-Baltistan. These reforms only strengthened the hold of Pakistan on this territory. The reforms gave the NA Council legislative, financial and executive powers. But it was a hoax because the same reforms vested financial and administrative powers in the Chief Executive, a Pakistani. The Deputy Chief Executive, a local based in Gilgit, could do only those things which the Chief Executive assigned to him. In the presence of the Pakistani Chief Executive there is no question of elected member daring to legislate.

A former policeman, Amir Hamza, who was eased out of his job because his wife made a speech in the NA Council critical of Pakistan's control over Gilgit-Baltistan, wrote an article in September 2002 in *K-2* (An Urdu magazine which is banned now because of its staunch nationalist views) that Pakistan does not trust the people of Gilgit-Baltistan. He wrote: "They (Pakistan Goverment) have never trusted us. From day one, i.e. November 1, 1947, till now we cannot govern our own land. If we are given that right, they think all hell will break loose."

As mentioned above Mr. Zulfikar Ali Bhutto had paved the way for political activities in Gilgit-Baltistan by scrapping FCR, which had outlawed political activities. His daughter Ms.

Bhutto became the first Pakistani Prime Minister to allow party based elections in Gilgit-Baltistan in October 1994. In these elections Pakistan-based parties the PPP, the Muslim League (Nawaz) and Shia religions party *Tehrik-i-Jafaria*, Pakistan (TJP), took part. Shias overwhelmingly voted for TJP and Shia independents. The Muslim League got only one seat because it was considered anti-Shia. (These elections were an eyewash as they did not allow the locals any real power to govern their own affairs).

Similarly, the conversion of the Judicial Commission into the Chief Court for the people of Gilgit-Baltistan by Ms. Bhutto did not inspire any confidence. The local people were not allowed to challenge its verdicts in Pakistani courts. The Chief Court has a retired judge of a Pakistani provincial court as its Chairman.

How meaningless these reforms were was clearly reflected in a verdict of Pakistan's Supreme Court on May 28, 1999 on the status of 'Northern Areas'. A full bench headed by Chief Justice, Justice Mr. Ajmal Mian ordered that the people of these areas be given all basic rights as provided in Pakistan's Constitution; that they should be allowed to run their own affairs through elected representatives, and that the constitution and rules be amended to provide independent judiciary to give them justice.

This judgment made it very clear that Pakistan's highest court was of the opinion that the NALC was not a representative body and the institution of the Chief Court was not credible.

Mr. Nawaz Sharif's government reacted to this judgment on July 14 when his Minister for Kashmir Affairs announced that a special committee would be constituted to prepare a constitutional package for 'Northern Areas' in the light of the Supreme Court's judgment. According to Urdu daily *Jang*,[3] Mr Nawaz Sharif's government had decided to give Gilgit and Baltistan a separate status like "AJK" and replace the Chief Court with a High Court. Mr. Sharif increased the number of

NALC seats from 26 to 30. 24 of these seats were to be filled through direct elections and the rest by the elected members of the Council.

The people had no faith in the Chief Court yet they were barred from approaching the High or Supreme Courts in Pakistan or POK. On October 5, 2005, Urdu BBC reported that the Court of Appeal was set-up in Gilgit today. It will have the same status as the Supreme Courts of Pakistan and POK. A judge of Peshawar High Court will be its Chief Justice.

In October 1990 two lawyers from Gilgit and Baltistan and one from POK filed a joint petition in POK's High Court pleading that, if Gilgit and Baltistan were part of the State of Jammu and Kashmir on August 15, 1947, then they should be reverted to the control of "AJK". They said the exclusion of Gilgit and Baltistan from "AJK" has resulted in depriving the residents of these areas from legitimate rights of representation in "Azad" Government, the Assembly, the Council and other institutions as well as basic rights and civil liberties. They also said that Gilgit and Baltistan were being administered without lawful authority. They prayed that the "Azad" government should be directed to take over the administration of the areas.

The Pakistan Government was named as a respondent. It challenged the High Court's jurisdiction saying it was confined to "AJK" only. Pakistan said Gilgit and Baltistan did not belong to it nor they belonged to "Azad" Kashmir. But it did not deny that Gilgit and Baltistan were part of the State of Jammu and Kashmir before August 15, 1947.

The High Court observed that the detachment of the Gilgit and Baltistan from the rest of "Azad" Jammu and Kashmir tantamounted to violation of the resolutions of the Security Council of March 30, 1951 and January 24, 1957.

It further said: "the State subjects residing in the 'Northern Areas' have been deprived of the benefits of fundamental rights, enshrined in the Interim Constitution Act (1974) during the past without lawful authority".

It said Pakistan had failed to explain why the residents of these areas have been kept deprived of the benefits of fundamental rights, civil liberties and the right of their representation in the government and other national institutions.

Pakistan chose not to reply to the Court's queries about the status of Gilgit and Baltistan before and on August 15, 1947 and about him who liberated these areas from Raja Hari Singh.

In its order dated March 8, 1993 the High Court accepted the petition and ordered:

i. a) The 'AJK' Government to immediately assume the administrative control of Gilgit and Baltistan and to annex it with administration of "AJK";

   b) The Government of Pakistan to provide adequate assistance and facility to the "AJK" Government in attainment of the said objective;

ii. The residents (state subjects) of Gilgit and Baltistan shall enjoy the benefits of fundamental rights conferred by the Act of 1974.

They shall be provided representation in:

1) the Government,

2) the Assembly,

3) the Council

4) Civil Services and

5) Other national institutions in due course of law.

iii. The "AJK" Government shall take steps to establish administrative and judicial set-up in Gilgit and Baltistan within the framework of the Interim Constitution Act.

The Pakistan Government appealed against this judgment in the POK Supreme Court. The Supreme Court in its order of September 14, 1994, said "Northern Areas" were part of the State of Jammu and Kashmir but are not part of POK as defined in the Interim Constitution Act. It negated the High Court's order.

However, the text of the High Court judgment clearly showed that the judges were not happy with Pakistan's control over Gilgit and Baltistan and its interference in POK's affairs. On the other hand, the POK Supreme Court in its judgment completely ignored the sad plight of the people of Gilgit and Baltistan.

As against the POK Supreme Court judgment Pakistan's Supreme Court judgment of May 29, 1999 expressed concern over the plight of the people of Gilgit and Baltistan. The court's judgment came in a petition which said that until the people get these rights they should not be asked to pay taxes and duties. If Gilgit and Baltistan are not part of Pakistan as Islamabad insisted, then the customs check posts should be removed to the territory of Pakistan and the locals should not be obstructed from carrying on trade with outside world, especially with China. All Pakistani laws except those concerning defence be abolished and Pakistani officials except defence personnel be called back.

Pakistan's reply to the Apex Court was: "Pakistan exercises *de facto* sovereignty over 'Northern Areas' with a view to complying with its obligations as a State under Public International Law, as well as a member of the United Nations Organization."

The Pakistan Government claimed that the people of Gilgit and Baltistan enjoyed civic amenities like health, education, transport, communication, law and order enforcement, issuance of Pakistani identity cards and passports.

The Pakistan Government claimed that it had the inalienable right to regulate such laws which might be deemed appropriate to earn revenues since it "expends huge amounts for the betterment of the people of 'Northern Areas' and on lubricating a vast administrative machinery."

Ground Realities

But Pakistani submission before the Suprement Court was full of exaggerations, as revealed from the following facts:

About 85 per cent of the 2 million strong population of Gilgit-Baltistan is Shia. They include 35 per cent Ismaili Shias. The Sunnis account for 15 per cent of the population. Most of them live in Diamer District. But since 1988 the complexion/demography of the population has been changing due to the influx of Sunni businessmen and others from Punjab and NWFP. Maharaja Hari Singh had banned entry and settlement of outsiders here. *The Friday Times*[4] has written that rapid settling of mostly Punjabi and Pakhtuns from outside, particularly the trading class, has created a sense of acute insecurity among the local Shias and has resulted in antagonistic perception between the locals and outsiders. As land prices rise and business flourishes in the hands of outsiders, there is a rush to grab scarce resources and opportunities in which the locals feel that they have been left out. Their lack of adequate political representation has only increased their sense of victimisation and discrimination.

The influx of outsiders has created two problems, depletion of employment opportunities for the locals and brutalisation of sectarian tension. Along with this there has come along a gun culture and the gradual replacement of spiritual values by crass materialism of the new middle class. The outsiders grab land and government jobs. It is not only the jobs that the outsiders grab, but also plunder their forest and natural resources. The funds allocated for the development of Gilgit and Baltistan are spent on the Army deployed there.

Local boys go to Pakistan to do menial jobs. There is a job quota for these boys but it is clubbed with Federally Administered Tribal Areas (FATA). FATA, because it has representation in Pakistan's Parliament, grabs most of the jobs. The unemployed boys from Gilgit and Baltistan are allegedly forced by ISI to fight in Kashmir.[5]

In his Urdu book, *Kaun Azad, Kaun Ghulam,* author Arif Shahid wrote in 1999 that many unemployed MAs and BAs had committed suicide. Low ranking Army officials from Gilgit and Baltistan end up as *chowkidars* after retirement for the bungalows of Pakistani Army officers.

Mr. Abdul Hamid Khan said in his letter to UNO that Pakistan officials smuggle drugs and arms between China and Pakistan through Karakoram Highway but locals are not allowed to carry on trade with China.

He also wrote that ISI had constructed torture chambers for the local leaders and nationalists who want independence.

Punishment for Being Shias

Until 1988 the people of Gilgit-Baltistan fought for their civil and democratic rights. In 1988 Gen Zia subverted their campaign by dividing the locals on sectarian lines. He also sent armed Sunni extremists to Gilgit-Baltistan to fight Shias. In the ensuing riots, hundreds of people, mostly Shias, were killed that year.

Today the Shias of Gilgit-Baltistan are not fighting so much for their democratic rights as for the protection of their faith. The school text books taught in Gilgit-Baltistan ignore Shia school of thought. Shia students protested but their peaceful protests failed to move the authorities. In May 2004, 2000 students went on a three-day hunger strike in Gilgit. Shia leaders supported the students. Thousands of Shias blocked roads and brought business activities to standstill. The Army came in and imposed curfew. Shias defied it and attacked the Frontier Constanbulary troops, Government buildings, police stations and vehicles. In Hunza they attacked one motel and set fire to the office of Assistant Commissioner. Gilgit was the nerve centre of agitations where thousands of agitators had converged.

Bhasha Dam

Pakistan's plan to build the Bhasha Dam has added to the long list of the grievances of the people of Gilgit-Baltistan. Gen. Musharraf announced this plan on January 17, 2006 when he had to drop his Kalabagh Dam Project under threats from Sindh. The people of Gilgit-Baltistan were shocked. They or the Northern Areas Council, were never told about it. Bhasha is a small village in Kohistan in NWFP. All the digging will be done in Diamer District submerging 30 villages and uprooting about 40,000 people. The entire Dam will be situated in Diamer yet it will be called Bhasha Dam. According to some experts, this is a trick to deprive Gilgit-Baltistan of royalty from the Dam. But nationalists argue that Pakistan has no right to build a Dam in a disputed territory.

Notes

1 *The Herald,* Karachi May 1990.

2 *The Friday Times,* October 15-21, 1992.

3 *Jang,* July 23, 1999

4 *The Friday Times,* October 15-21, 1992

5 This is disclosed in a letter to UNO by Chairman of Balwaristan Front Abdul Hamid Khan in 1997. Balwaristan is a name given to Northern Areas by the nationalists.

8

How Azad is 'Azad Kashmir': An Analysis of Relations between Islamabad and Muzaffarabad

Smruti S Pattanaik

The Kashmir issue has been the lynchpin of Pakistan's contested nationhood. The question of accession of Kashmir has become one of the controversial issues that Pakistan, without any legal stand, is contesting. It has entirely based its argument on two-nation theory and feels that Kashmir, being a Muslim majority state, should rightly belong to Pakistan. In the conference of the state rulers and their representatives, Mountbatten, referring to the Indian Independence Act, said on July 25, 1947, that it "releases the states from their obligation to the Crown. The states have complete freedom technically and legally they are independent...you cannot run away from the Dominion government which is your neighbour any more than you can run away from the subjects for whose welfare you are responsible".[1] It also needs to be emphasized that it was the British India that was to be divided on the basis of two-nation theory. This is evident from the fact that in September 1944, Jinnah, while replying to Gandhi's enquiry on the status of the Lahore resolution wrote: "it is confined to British India"[2]. Moreover, the relations between the British India and the princely states were governed by a different set of rules. With the partition of India, the question of accession of princely states became crucial. Accession of three princely states was contested by India and Pakistan. Giving scant regard to territorial contiguity, Pakistan had accepted the accession of Junagarh even when the majority of the subject population was Hindus. In fact Jinnah even supported the accession of Junagarh to Pakistan on the basis that the ruler's decision is final. To quote Jinnah, "Constitutionally and legally, the Indian states will be independent sovereign states on the termination of paramountcy and they will be free to decide for themselves and to adopt any course they like; it is open to them to join the Hindustan Constituent Assembly or the Pakistan Constituent Assembly, or decide to remain independent....The policy of the All India Muslim League has been clear from the very beginning; we do not wish to interfere with the internal affairs of any State. For that is a matter primarily to be resolved between the rulers and the people of the States".[3] Pakistan that was created on the basis of two-nation theory has laid its claim on Kashmir only on the basis of this. It needs to be emphasized that British India led by the Indian National Congress during the time of partition did not subscribe to the two-nation theory and accepted it as *fait accompli*. As India adopted multi-culturalism and secularism as the basis of its nationhood, it challenged the very notion of Pakistan's nationhood based on religion.

The accession of Kashmir to India on the eve of tribal raid played catalyst to the irresolute political allegiance of the erstwhile Maharaja. Hari Singh, the ruler of Kashmir signed the instrument of accession to India leading India to take over the security of the entire state. India sent its troops to Kashmir to protect the state from the invasion of Pakistan instigated tribes with the active participation of its armed forces. The Muslim soldiers of Maharaja's force and the Gilgit Scouts, with the connivance of some British officers, captured the Northern areas of Gilgit and Baltistan and declared their accession to Pakistan. This area was leased to the British and had reverted to the Maharaja as the British paramountcy over the princely state lapsed. The areas that Pakistan refers to as 'Azad Kashmir' 'AJK', were under the Maharaja's rule during the British period. The reference denotes to the area 'liberated' by the tribes and disguised armed forces personnel and essentially does not constitute the entire territory of Pakistan Occupied Kashmir (POK).[4] Therefore it needs to be kept in mind that 'Azad Kashmir' is only a part of POK and Gilgit and Baltistan which exist under the nomenclature of 'Northern Areas' is a legitimate part of the territory of the state of Jammu and Kashmir. Often some scholars make the mistake of confusing 'Azad Kashmir' with Pakistan Occupied Kashmir.[5] The focus of the paper is confined to the relations between the 'Azad Kashmir' and the state of Pakistan. The description 'Azad' or liberated is a stance that Pakistan has taken from the perspective of its national identity construction. Since Pakistan claims that it is the embodiment of the sub-continent Muslims' political and economic aspirations, it has taken upon itself the role of a spokesperson of the Muslims. By portraying the part of the occupied Kashmir as 'Azad', Pakistan projects it as a logical culmination of the Muslims of Kashmir joining the 'land of pure'. The relation between Islamabad and Muzaffarabad is like a feudal and his *haris*. The former not only controls but directs and is responsible for latter's survival and sustenance. In fact only those political parties in 'Azad Kashmir' that support state's accession to Pakistan are allowed to function. They also compete and vie with one another for Islamabad's political patronage for their survival in power in Muzaffarabad, the capital of the 'AJK'.

By portraying part of the Kashmir that is under Pakistan's occupation as 'Azad', Pakistan has also built up an opinion that the Gilgit-Baltistan is not a part of the Kashmir dispute. Therefore it is not surprising that while discussing the issue of Kashmir many Pakistani analysts feel a little reluctant to speak about the status of the 'Northern Areas'.[6] This was also evident in Gen Musharraf's interview with Indian journalist Karan

Thapar. While replying to Thapar's question whether he would give self-governance to 'Northern Areas' he paused before he said "we would like to give them self-governance".

'Azad Kashmir' and Gilgit-Baltistan have been kept separately from each other so that dissatisfaction regarding their political rights and economic well-being can be contained and also to prevent a consolidated movement to emerge which could challenge the Pakistani state's control over the POK. The 'Northern Areas' is not a province of Pakistan and is governed by the Ministry of Kashmir and Northern Areas Affairs (KANA). Till 1972, it was ruled by the Frontier Crime Regulation (FCR) through the Ministry of Kashmir and Frontier Affairs. It was only in 1994 the federal government allowed the political parties of Pakistan to function in 'Northern Areas' but it did not allow the parties from 'Azad Kashmir' to operate there. Gilgit and Baltistan have been made political scapegoat for the ultimate solution of the Kashmir. issue. Pakistan is reluctant to extend them a formal Pakistani citizenship because it fears that accepting them as Pakistani citizens would lead to the formalization of LoC as an international border. In September 2004 when the citizenship identity cards were issued they did not mention that the people are citizens of 'AJK' leading to widespread protests by the JK National Students Federation and All Parties National Alliance.

Pakistan has tried to politically situate the so-called 'AJK' differently from the 'Northern Areas'. This inevitably confines the territorial limits of the conflict only to the 'AJK'. In fact by giving trappings of independence to various political denominations that are in place in the 'AJK', the Pakistani government tries to create an allusion of independence to camouflage the nature of its political status. It has controlled the political voice and has encouraged Islamabad stooges to hold on to power. The Pakistan state has been able to successfully divert the attention of the world to the Indian part of Kashmir. The problem also arises from the fact that there is hardly any scholarly attention to the politico-social structure of the 'AJK' and the media in Pakistan does not focus on the socio-economic developments there. As one understands, the media focus has only been on the happenings in the Indian part of Kashmir without any news on the political developments in the 'AJK'. As a result an impression is created that everything is fine with the 'AJK' and Gilgit-Baltistan. Only recently, Pakistan media, due to trouble in Gilgit-Baltistan, is focusing on the state of affairs there. Absence of well researched publication has helped the government of Pakistan to conceal the political developments and protect it from being probed. Therefore, there is a need to focus on the political and economic developments in 'AJK', to analyse the state of socio-economic well being and also the political relations between Islamabad and Muzaffarabad.

The extent of independence of 'AJK' can be gauged from the fact that Pakistan ceded part of the territory of Kashmir to China without consulting the Kashmiris. Pakistan is reluctant to hand over the Gilgit-Baltistan to 'AJK' because it has the strategic Karakoram Highway passing through this area and has a major military base in Skardu. It portrays Maharaja's Muslim armed personnel's revolt in Gilgit-Baltistan as reflection of a popular expression of will, therefore, claims the accession is complete. The construction of Mangla Dam which is benefiting the Punjab province displaced many Kashmiris especially the Mirpuris who are right now settled outside and this has also been a major bone of contention.

Gilgit and Baltistan, which are legally part of the princely state of Kashmir have been kept aside and the administration is managed by the State of Pakistan through its Minister of KANA. The Chief Justice of the 'Azad Kashmir' High Court, on a writ petition filed on October 16, 1990 by a number of Kashmiris, observed in its judgment on March 8, 1993 that the 'Northern Areas' are part of the state of Jammu and Kashmir as it existed on August 15, 1947 and detachment of Gilgit-Baltistan from the 'Azad Kashmir' is illegal. It directed the 'AJK' government to set up all executive and judicial institutions in those areas as per the interim constitution of 1974. Interestingly, the court observed that though the government of Pakistan has opined that the 'AJK' High Court has no power to hear these writ petitions, the Court said that the point of judicial jurisdiction was, however, executed in detail under the 'AJK' government's interim constitution of 1974. It finally observed that the court has full powers not only to pass verdict on such petition but also to hear all matters relating to the entire state. The court further said the powers vested in the government of Pakistan under the interim constitution are also liable to be reviewed by the 'AJK' High Court. However, this judgment was overturned by the 'Azad Kashmir' Supreme Court saving Pakistan government from further embarrassment.

The Preamble to the 'AJK' constitution reads "The status of 'AJK' is that of 'local authority' as envisaged in the UN Resolution. The Local authority is clarified by the Commission to mean people of 'AJK' who shall have full political and Administrative control over the evacuated territories"[7]. Pakistan had constituted provisional J&K government in Poonch after occupying it with M.R Ibrahim of Muslim Conference as its provisional head. Pakistan's conferment of the status of local authority was contested by India and the UNCIP resolution took due note of India's protest. This is one of the reasons why it insisted on the withdrawal of Pakistan troops to be communicated to India. The preamble further defines 'AJK' as "territories of the state of Jammu and Kashmir which have been liberated by the people of that state and for the time being under the administration of Government and such other territories as may come under its administration". This provision itself tries to portray that the part of the state was "liberated" by its own people. The UN resolution which Pakistan cites to buttress its demand for plebiscite clearly mentions that Pakistan needs to withdraw tribesman and other forces which have entered the state unlawfully.[8] The involvement of Pakistan Army in the so-called tribal raids into Kashmir has been documented by Maj Gen Akbar Khan of Pakistan Army.[9]

Socio-Economic Profile

Less than half of the budgetary expenses of the state is financed by the 'AJK' government from the local taxes it collects. Rest is financed by the federal government from the share of 'AJK' from federal tax, royalties from the power generated from the Mangla Dam, share of tax collected from the 'AJK' territories. The 'AJK' government also remains heavily dependent on foreign aid for most of its development schemes, which include new roads, schools, hospitals, drinking water facilities and improvement in the region's electricity infrastructure.[10] All the funding from the foreign agencies is channelled through Islamabad. Due to poor planning half of the fund remains unutilized in the 'AJK'. For example: in July 1997, the government departments were asked to ensure 65 per cent utilization of their allocations by the end of the third quarter. It also warned that if the funds are not utilized within the time frame, the unused funds would be transferred to departments requiring additional funds.[11]

Islam is declared as the state religion. This is not surprising because Pakistan's entire claim is based on religion which has little political, economic and social space for the minorities. The state of Jammu and Kashmir is multi-ethnic and multi-religious. Introduction of state religion itself attests to the fact that other religions would not have same right. The state subjects are classified into four classes. Class I are all persons born and residing within the state before the commencement of the reign of His Highness the late Maharaja Gulab Singh and who settled therein before the commencement of Samvat year 1942 and have since been permanently residing. Class II are those who settled before the close of Samvat year 1968 and are residing permanently and have acquired immovable property, Class III are the people who under *rayatnama* have acquired immovable property and may hereafter acquire such property under *ijatnama* and may execute a *rayatnama* after ten year. Class IV are Companies which provide economic benefit to the state and by special order of His Highness have been declared as the state subjects. The state subject is under the purview of the Council. It does not impose any restriction on the settlement of the people of other parts of Pakistan in the state. In a judgment the 'AJK' High Court observed "the Council was fully empowered to make laws concerning citizenship for territories of Azad Jammu and Kashmir and there was no embargo on its powers to enact a law pertaining to citizenship or domicile in respects of persons residing or having a domicile in Azad Kashmir".[12] It needs to be mentioned here that the Council has majority of its members representing the federal government in Islamabad. The powers to issue a certificate of state subject are delegated to District Magistrate of all the districts of 'Azad Jammu and Kashmir'.

Constitutional Developments: Playing with Semantics

The Preamble to the constitution of 'AJK' reads "The state of Jammu and Kashmir under the instrument of partition should have formed the part of Pakistan, as majority rather predominant part of its population, is Muslims". This presumption underlines Islamabad's approach and it defines its stand on Kashmir. However, this is extremely misleading and is in contravention to the principle of partition of British India. As already mentioned, it was the British India that was partitioned on the basis of two-nation theory. The princely states did not come under the purview of communal partition. Interestingly Pakistan considers the government of 'Azad Kashmir' is constituted as per the UN resolution. For example the 1974 interim constitution under the subheading "provisions for better Government and Administration of liberated territories of the State of Jammu and Kashmir" reads: "The status of Azad Jammu and Kashmir is that of a 'local authority' as envisaged by the United Nations Resolution. The local authority is clarified by the Commission, to mean people of Azad Jammu and Kashmir who shall have full Political and Administrative control of the evacuated territories."[13] The 'AJK' is projected as the successor state of Maharaja representing the entire state of J&K.[14] As per the UN Resolutions: "The Government of Pakistan will use its best endeavour to secure the withdrawal from the State of Jammu and Kashmir, of tribesmen and Pakistan nationals not normally resident therein who have entered the State for the purpose of fighting." It further stated that "Pending a final solution, the territory evacuated by the Pakistani troops will be administered by the local authorities under the surveillance of the Commission". Pakistan wanted to project the 'Azad Kashmir' government as local authority. In fact to have a decisive control over the 'Azad Kashmir' it created 'Northern Areas' as separate entity as per the 1949 Karachi Agreement (See Appendix-1) and stationed its troops there. So it could escape the UNCIP resolution of withdrawing troops from the entire area occupied by it. Pakistan currently has its troops stationed both on the sensitive 'Northern Areas' and the 'AJK'. As mentioned earlier, 'Northern Areas' is not considered as liberated territory[15] as it was leased to the British till 1947.

The 1949 Karachi agreement signed between Pakistan and 'Azad Kashmir' government limited the role of the government of 'Azad Kashmir' to that of a client state. It also separated the 'Northern Areas' from the purview of 'Azad Kashmir' government. It equated the Muslim Conference party with that of the government of 'AJK'. (See Appendix-I) Pakistan was ruling 'AJK' through a Joint Secretary responsible to the ministry of KANA. From 1948 to 1970 the Joint Secretary played an important role in representing the military government in Islamabad. It patronaged the Muslim Conference as per the Karachi Agreement. In fact the Muslim Conference was an ally of Muslim League in pre-partition India as National Conference was close to the Indian National Congress.

In 1950 Pakistan tried to piece together a semblance of government in 'AJK'. The rules of business passed that year provided for a president and a council consisting of the president and ministers. It also had a 'Supreme Head' who appointed the president, and the council along with the president remained responsible to the Supreme Head. For a long time the position of Supreme Head was occupied by the president of the Muslim Conference. The rules of business of the 'Azad Kashmir' government define the Supreme Head as the "Head of the Azad Kashmir Movement". This order made the Muslim Conference synonymous with the state exactly on the same line as that of the Muslim League's relations with the Federal government in the formative years of Pakistan. The Council had the power to sanction the appointment of gazetted officers and look into the administration.

In 1952, rules of business for 'Azad Kashmir' Government was introduced which clearly stated that the President of 'AJK' shall hold office during the pleasure of General Council of the All Jammu Kashmir Muslim Conference duly recognized as such by the Government of Pakistan in the Ministry of Kashmir Affairs. The legislative functions of the 'AJK' were made subservient to the state of Pakistan through the Ministry of Kashmir Affairs. For example the legislative function of the state reads: "Supreme Legislative power shall vest in the Council provided that no draft legislation shall be put before the Council without obtaining the advice of the Ministry of Kashmir Affairs thereon, and in case it is proposed to come to a decision at variance with such advice it shall not be given effect to without prior consultation with the Ministry of Kashmir Affairs." It further added that "Legislation or rules having the force of law, after receiving the concurrence of the Ministry of Kashmir Affairs shall be published in the Government Gazette and shall then deemed to have come into force on such date as specified thereon."[16] The Ministers did not even have the right to transfer the gazetted officers without the concurrence of the President of the 'AJK'. Interestingly functions of the Joint Secretary were defined as: "In addition to general supervision over all departments of government, the Joint Secretary, Ministry of Kashmir Affairs shall pass final orders on appeals against orders passed by Secretaries and Head of

Departments in respect of Government servants under their control in matters of appointments, promotion and disciplinary action of all kinds." This makes it clear that the state was ruled by a Joint Secretary who was in the supervision of all the departments in AJK, so much for the independence. It was further stated: "The ministry of Kashmir affairs shall have general supervision over the Azad Kashmir government in matters of policy and general administration." This put the administration under the control of the Federal government of Pakistan.

The agenda to be discussed in the Council is decided by Islamabad. The Secretary General issues to the Ministry of Kashmir Affairs an agenda showing the cases to be discussed at least one week before the meeting. The Secretary General not only attends all the Council meetings but all the orders of the Council need to be authenticated by the Secretary General or the Deputy Secretary General. The joint secretary of the Ministry of Kashmir Affairs can attend any of the meetings and tender advice on any matters that is under discussion. It was also required that the advice of Ministry of Kashmir Affairs would be obtained before some of the subjects are submitted to the council.[17] In Nov 1958, after Ayub Khan assumed power he brought certain changes to the rules of business for the 'AJK' government. The Chief Advisor who was an officer appointed by the Ministry of Kashmir Affairs however, remained supreme. The rules of business of 'AJK' define "Chief Adviser means the officer so appointed or in his absence the officer who has been allowed by the Ministry of Kashmir Affairs to work on his behalf". This order separated the advice that the government needed to seek from the Kashmir Affairs Ministry[18] from the ones where the permission needed to be sought from the Chief Advisor. For the first time it said: "All important matters requiring advice of the Ministry of Kashmir Affairs would be put to the Minister-in-Charge and the President as the case may be, for their concurrence before reference to the Ministry of Kashmir Affairs." This order also mentioned that on matters pertaining to any recurring or non-recurring expenditure up to the extent of Rs one lac per annum from the budget provision or to create a post carrying a pay not exceeding Rs. 150 per month (without allowances) the decision could be taken by the government of 'AJK' without referring it to the Kashmir Affairs Ministry.

The Basic Democrat Act was extended to the 'AJK' in 1960. However, the power relations between Islamabad and Muzafarabad remained the same. During Gen Ayub's regime Kashmir was regarded as personal fiefdom of the Pakistanis "...the powerbrokers in Azad Kashmir and the bureaucrats in Rawalpindi who saw Azad Kashmir – hypocritically described as the 'forward camp' of the entire State's liberation— as no more than personal fiefdom...". It was "considered quite normal that Azad Kashmir chief executives should wait outside the Joint Secretary's office before being called in".[19] The basic democrat system provided for Presidential system of government and an 'AJK' Council. The Council consisted of 24 members, 12 each elected by the 'AJK' basic democrats and 12 from among the refugees. The Chief Advisor retained the power to nominate the Chairman of the Council and he also acted as the ex-officio President of the 'AJK'.

Cosmetic political changes were adopted as the relationship of a patron and client continued between Islamabad and Muzaffarabad. Pakistan government in 1964 brought in the 'AJK' Act. Under the new Act the Chairman was deemed to be a member of State Council if he was not a member. The State Council could not remove the Chairman without the written consent of the Advisor. The Chief Advisor, an Islamabad appointee, would also appoint a person to be the Secretary to the State Council. The State Council could not enact any law pertaining to (i) the organization, discipline and control of the armed forces (ii) evacuee property (iii) the provisions pertaining to the 'AJK' government Act or the rules made thereunder and their repeal and modification. In 1964, the government brought in another amendment to the 1964 Act.

It defined the Chief Advisor as "an officer appointed by the Azad government of the State of Jammu and Kashmir on the advice of the Government of Pakistan to be the Chief Advisor to the Government". It is important to mention here that earlier the Chief Advisor was appointed by the Government of Pakistan. The 'AJK' government had no role in it. Even if the clause gave a semblance of power to the 'AJK' government, it amounted to playing with the semantics. The government of Pakistan still retained its power to play an important role in the appointment of the Chief Advisor. Similarly changes were brought to the appointment of the Chairman of the council. Instead of any person, the Chief Advisor in consultation with the State Council nominated one of its members as Chairman or if it deemed fit, after consultation with the council, could appoint any other person as the Chairman. However, such person needed to be elected within six months of his nomination. Later the Act of 1965 brought some superficial changes.

In 1968 the size of the State Council was increased. Now the State Council constituted of eight members to be elected through the system of basic democrats and four members to be nominated by the Chief Advisor from the refugees residing in Pakistan. The allowances of the members could be determined by the Government of 'AJK' with the concurrence of the Chief Advisor. It also stipulated that a Chairman could be elected from amongst its members. The Chairman would ex-officio be the President of the 'AJK'. The President of 'AJK' in consultation with the Chief Advisor could make law through ordinances when the Council was not in session or suspended or on a subject on which the State Council could not make a law. The 'AJK' Act of 1969 made some changes to the 1968 Act. It stated if the Chairman's seat was vacant for any reason the Chief Advisor would nominate a person as the Chairman. Instead of choosing a member of the State Council who is qualified to be elected as the Chairman, it substituted it with 'a person'. The 1969 Act also made changes to section 20 that dealt with the election of the Chairman of the council, the words 'or nominated' was inserted to the earlier provision that only talked of 'elected'.

The 'Azad' Jammu Kashmir Government Act of 1970 for the first time stipulated an elected President. In any case Pakistan itself did not have any direct elections till 1970. The Azad Kashmiris were given the right of adult franchise to participate in the election under Yahya regime. However, the President, before he entered the office, needed to take an oath affirming his allegiance to the state's accession to Pakistan under the 'AJK' Oath of Office Ordinance specified in the Schedule 1. A plebiscite advisor would be appointed by the president in consultation with the Advisor (earlier Chief Advisor). It stipulated a twenty-five members Legislative Assembly out of which twenty-four would be directly elected and one women member would be elected by the directly elected members. It also mentioned that the government could not spend beyond the approved budget and "no expenditure on such major development activities as may be specified by the Advisor shall be incurred except with the approval of the Advisor". This clearly indicates that even the 'AJK' government could not undertake developmental activities without the approval of the Chief Advisor, an appointee of Islamabad.

The 1974 interim constitution brought in major changes to the 'AJK'. It established parliamentary form of representation in line with Pakistan. The 'AJK' council was created and given executive and legislative authority. It also created a joint sitting of the Council, the Assembly and the Federal Minister in charge of the council secretariat, which would deal with the election and removal of the President (Section 5 & 6), Amendments in the Constitution (Section 33) and consideration of proclamations issued under Section 53 to be laid within thirty days of issuance. As per Section 21, 'AJK' council consists of the Prime Minister of Pakistan, the President of 'AJK', five members nominated by the Prime Minister of Pakistan from among the Federal Ministers and the members of Parliament, the PM of 'AJK' or a person nominated by him and six members to be elected by the Assembly from amongst the State Subjects in accordance with the system of proportional representation by means of single transferable vote. The Prime Minister of Pakistan shall be the Chairman of the Council, the President is the Vice-Chairman. The Federal Minister of State for Kashmir and Northern Areas shall be ex-officio member of the Council. This was inserted by Act VII of 1976. The President of 'AJK' can be elected through "members of the joint sitting by votes of majority of the total membership of the Joint Sitting" and he can be removed by two-thirds of the total membership of the joint sitting. This provision clearly establishes the fact that if the Assembly members decide to abstain a President can be elected and sacked by Islamabad's representative. The most important aspect of this is that its decision is final and cannot be challenged in any court.

It is important to mention here that the government of Pakistan began to have a more direct role in the matters of 'AJK' after the1972 Simla Agreement. Though it gave a façade of independence by providing for the President and the Prime Minister its relations were more open and direct. As many analysts and some of them who had played important role during the Simla agreement, believe that this formalization was the outcome of the understanding between Bhutto and Mrs Indira Gandhi. Changes were also brought in Gilgit-Baltistan which came under a direct rule rather than being governed by Frontier Crime Regulation Act. The Ministry of Kashmir and Frontier Affairs was changed to Ministry of Kashmir Affairs and Northern Areas. The restriction on state subjects and buying of property in Gilgit and Baltistan was withdrawn and people from any area of Pakistan now could buy property and settle down in the region. Islamabad appoints an administrative head to look into the local affairs. Most of the time, this post is occupied by a retired Army officer.

Qualifying the Political Contenders

The function of the political parties is governed by Section 33 of the 'AJK' Act, which states that "no person or political party in Azad Jammu and Kashmir shall be permitted to propagate against or take part in activities prejudicial or detrimental to the ideology of the State's accession to Pakistan". Article 5 (b) section (vii) of the 'AJK' Legislative Assembly Election Ordinance 1970, which is still in place, states that a member will be disqualified from contesting the election if "he is propagating any opinion or action in any manner, prejudicial to the ideology of Pakistan, or the sovereignty, integrity of Pakistan or security of Azad Jammu and Kashmir or Pakistan or morality or the maintenance of public order or the integrity or independence of the judiciary of Azad Jammu and Kashmir or Pakistan or who defames or brings into ridicule the judiciary of Azad Jammu and Kashmir or Pakistan or the Armed Forces of Pakistan". Sub clause 2 of sub section 7 of section 4 puts an embargo upon all individuals and political parties "not to propagate or take part in activities prejudicial or detrimental to, the ideology of the State's accession to Pakistan. The future status of the State of J&K is yet to be determined in accordance with the freely expressed wishes of the votes of the people till then, the ideology of State's accession to Pakistan is final and the same cannot be questioned". The Political Parties Act under Section 9 prohibits and recommends dissolution of any party that "propagates any idea other than the accession of the State to Pakistan". This provision of finality of accession attests to the fact that 'AJK' government is not a 'local authority' as Pakistan claims it to be under the UNCIP resolution.

The 'AJK' interim constitution of 1970, Section 4(7ii) says "no person or political party in 'AJK' shall be permitted to propagate against or take part in activities prejudicial or detrimental to the ideology of the state's accession to Pakistan". This reflects the restriction on political activities and exercise of control over the political will of the people and confining it to state's accession to Pakistan rather than giving them scope to exercise the options available to them under the UN resolutions, which Pakistan so vociferously advocates. After coercing people to support state's accession to Pakistan, it is not surprising that Pakistan speaks of plebiscite even when it makes it mandatory for the political parties and people to exercise their political rights with a condition.[20] The state subjects cannot criticize the territory's incorporation into Pakistan, cannot demand the reunification of Gilgit and Baltistan with 'AJK', cannot advocate independence as an option, cannot criticise the partition of India and can not criticise the Pakistan armed forces.

'AJK' has many political parties functioning in the state. The national parties clearly have their own mandate and their approaches are appendage to the objectives of the national parties. Some of the local political parties are concerned with local issues. The Muslim Conference that dominated the politics of 'AJK' had close relations with the Muslim League. In fact Muslim Conference was formed in opposition to the National Conference in pre-partition era and obviously it had to propagate the Muslim League's views based on two-nation theory in Kashmir. After the 'AJK' came into being the Muslim Conference played an important role. It emerged as the sole spokesperson for the Kashmiris on the Pakistani side albeit with Islamabad's authorization and scrutiny.

During Ayub's regime, with the introduction of basic democrats, political parties were not allowed. It was only in 1985, the political parties were allowed to contest elections although the elections for the National Assembly of Pakistan were held on non-party basis. However, the participation of political parties was regulated. The pro-Pakistan leaders in 'AJK' wanted to put some conditions to please Islamabad. As a result two ordinances were promulgated in April 1985 which clearly stated that the registration of political parties would be cancelled if they poll less than 12.5 per cent of total valid votes cast, and less than 5 per cent of the aggregate of the valid votes in each district, besides cancellation of its elected members from being members of the Assembly. This decision was challenged by the political parties in the High Court as infringement of fundamental rights. However, the High Court in a majority view said "Operation of Section 8-A of the 1985 Ordinance, which suspends functioning of political activities of political parties, abridges basic right – Fact that political parties participated in election and captured certain seats and now by operation of Section 8-A, or Ordinance of 1985, political parties are to lose those seats". Losing of seats cannot be called infringement of fundamental right. However, "To deprive a political party of its representation in Assembly is tantamount to hamper and abridge fundamental right – Such legislation clearly violates constitution".[21] The court also said that the restriction to secure 12 per cent of aggregate votes and 5 per cent from each district after the announcement of elections is a bad law. This is because there was no popular demand to introduce such a system nor was there any urgency at the national level to justify its enforcement. It also said that none of the political parties were in a position to adjust to conditions created by the system and no safeguards were provided to political parties. This ordinance was brought keeping in mind the Pakistan Peoples Party (PPP) and allowed the Muslim Conference to win making Sardar Sikandar Hayat as the Prime Minister and Sardar Qayyum Khan as the President. Pakistan has been conducting farcical elections in 'Azad Kashmir' and has instituted its puppets in the state. The farcical nature of the post of Prime Minister can be gauged from the fact that in 1991, the Chief Secretary of 'Azad Kashmir' government who is a direct appointee of Islamabad ordered the arrest of Mumtaz Hussain Rathore who was then the so-called Prime Minister of the 'AJK', for his anti-Pakistan remark, calling for real freedom in the state. Interestingly, the 1991 elections that were marked by violence saw the 'AJK' Muslim Conference emerging victorious and this led Rathore (PPP) to declare the election invalid leading to his arrest in Islamabad.

The pro-independence parties have never been allowed to participate in the election as they refused to take oath under the constitution to work for the state's accession to Pakistan. In 2005, Sardar Sikandal Hayat Khan called for repeal of all those amendments that "put a bar on the authority of the AJK government....to safeguard the identity of the state". On May 20, 2005, the speaker of 'AJK' government appointed a seven member committee to propose amendments to the 1974 constitution. The committee is yet to came up with its recommendations and the 2006 elections took place with the condition that the candidate had to swear his allegiance to the state's accession to Pakistan. The spokesperson of the foreign office in the 2006 election defended the government's position to reject the nomination papers of pro independence candidates by saying 'AJK' elections are governed by the constitution of AJK. The elections are not controlled by Pakistan. If there's a column on accession (in the nomination papers), it is in 'AJK' constitution, not in the Pakistan constitution. The 'AJK' constitution has been drafted by their own leaders.[23] Around 30 nomination papers each of the JKLF and All Party National Alliance candidates were rejected by the election commission. The JKLF leader Sardar Saghir Khan, who is also its General Secretary, reacting to the foreign office spokesperson's statement, said that the preamble to the constitution states that the document was approved by the government of Pakistan which had authorized the 'AJK' government to introduce it to their legislature for their approval. Therefore, it is not true to say that this qualification is approved by their own government as Islamabad's control over the legislature of the 'AJK' is total.

The issue of Kashmir has been hijacked from the political parties of 'AJK', instead various jihadi organizations have been encouraged to pursue Pakistan's agenda in Kashmir. There has been immense dissatisfaction, as Pakistan has never given the political parties a say in the resolution of Kashmir issue while encouraging the Indian Hurriyat and portraying them as sole representative of the Kashmiris. In fact ISI at one point of time had funded and armed the JKLF. Amanullah Khan, the chief of JKLF has said "I remembered Gen Zia had once said that he wanted Kashmir to become member of the Organisation of Islamic Conference, which clearly meant independent Kashmir."[24] Due to its pro-independence stance the JKLF soon got disillusioned with Pakistani policy and ISI also stopped supporting them.

The 'AJK' has remained under the effective control of Islamabad. In spite of the 'AJK' having its own Assembly, the law made by the Council has prevailed. The Council has not only had exclusive right to legislate on important matters pertaining to the governance of the 'AJK' but also has the executive power over the legislative list (see Appendix-2). The Pakistan government has exclusive powers pertaining to its responsibility under UNCIP resolution, currency notes and coins, external affairs of the 'AJK' including foreign aid and trade. The 'AJK' government has not played any role in the Kashmir issues. At the same time the Pakistan government has tried to utilize the Srinagar based Hurriyat Conference to project them as representative of Kashmiri opinion. Though it has always argued for a plebiscite in Kashmir, it has not maintained the original ethnic balance in the Pakistan occupied Kashmir. Islamabad has tried to marginalize the Kashmiris and has a strict control over their budget. The façade of independence continues under the jackboot of Pakistan's occupation.

Notes.

[1] Pandrel Moon, (ed), *The Transfer of power 1942-47*, vol.XII London: HMSO, n.d., pp.348-351.

[2] Cited in DALow (ed), *The political inheritance of Pakistan*, London: Macmillan, 1991, p.221.

[3] The Indian Annual Register, 1947, p.112 as cited in Damodar R. Sar Desai, "The Origins of Kashmir's International and Legal

Status" in Raju GC Thomas (ed), *Perspectives on Kashmir: The Roots of Conflict in South Asia* Boulder: Westview Press, 1992, p.83.

4 It is important to mention here that the term Pakistan occupied Kashmir has been used as the legality of the state's accession to India is a valid legal document and draws its validity from the British rules regarding the lapse of Paramountacy.

5 Even Scholar like Leo E Rose has used reference Azad Kashmir or Pakistan occupied Kashmir alternatively in his paper on the subject. Leo E Rose, "The Politics of Azad Kashmir" in Raju GC Thomas (ed), *Perspectives in Kashmir,* Westview Press, 1992, p.236.

6 This is based on my interviews carried in Pakistan in January-February, 2001.

7 Syed Manzoor H Gilani, *Constitutional Development in AJK,* Muzaffarabad: National Book Depot, 1988, p.27.

8 Emphasis is mine. A1 and 2 of the 1948 UN resolutions.

9 Akbar Khan, *Raiders in Kashmir,* Delhi: Army Publishers, n.d.

10 "The AJK Budget", Editorial *Dawan,* June 21, 2005

11 "Half of the AJK Development Allocation Remains Unutilized", *Dawn,* April 29, 2004.

12 Gilani, n.7, p.41.

13 Ibid., p.27.

14 Ibid., p.28.

15 For details regarding the so-called revolution see Brig. Ghansar Singh Jamwal, *"Gilgit Before 1947: A Memoir",* Delhi: Sarasawti Printers, n.d., pp.23-40.

16 Gilani n. 7, p.79.

17 All questions of General policy, (b) all important matters involving heavy financial commitments on the government level, all matters relating to legislation, enactment of statutory rules, regulations and by laws requiring the sanction of the council, (c) state Budget (d) alienation of state Property (e) internal security (f) public debts and loans (g) foreign relations etc., Ibid., p.102.

18 The issues on which the government needs to seek are (i) state Budget (ii) Public Debts and Loans (iii) Foreign Relations (iv) Town Improvement and Development Schemes (v) Levy of new taxes and abolishing of existing ones. The advice of Chief Secretary shall be obtained on the following matters before it being submitted to the state council. (i) All matters relating to legislation, enactment of statutory rules, regulations and by laws requiring the sanction of the Council, (ii) Alienation of State property (iii) Internal Security (iv) All important mattes relating to civil supplies and rehabilitation (v) All forest schemes, leases and contracts exceeding the value of Rs 1,00,000. (vi) Important matters relating tö evacuees and evacuee property.

19 Khalid Hasan (ed), *K.H.Khurshid: Memoirs of Jinnah,* Dhaka: UPL, 1990, p. xiv.

20 For example, in the election of 1991 to Legislative Assembly a person named Aftab Hussain, a JKLF sympathizer, while filing his nomination paper deleted the words which declares his allegiance to "the ideology of Pakistan, the ideology of State's accession to Pakistan and the integrity and sovereignty of Pakistan" and wrote "freedom of Jammu and Kashmir." As a result his nomination paper was rejected by the returning officer. The 'AJK' High court in its ruling in August 1991 upheld the decision of returning officer and said the word 'freedom' for the state subjects' means freedom from India but it did not mean freedom from Pakistan. Its accession to Pakistan is legal and constitutional.

21 Gilani, n.7, p.75.

22 Ibid, p.77.

23 Nirupama Subramaniun, "We have no Role in 'AJK' Poll", *The Hindu,* June 14, 2006.

24 Zulfiqar Ali, "For the Record", *The Herald,* July 2005, p.55.

Appendix-I

Text of the agreement signed between Pakistan and Azad Kashmir Governments in March 1949. The Agreement was signed by the following:

1. Honourable Mushtaque Ahmed Gurmani, Minister without Portfolio, Government of Pakistan.
2. Sardar Mohammed Ibrahim Khan, the President of Azad Kashmir.
3. Choudhry Ghulam Abbas, Head of All Jammu and Kashmir Muslim Conference.

This was the only Kashmiri political party on this side of the cease fire line at that time, and the Agreement it was persuaded to sign, very seriously limited the role of Azad Kashmir Government in the Kashmiri freedom struggle. Therefore, it is no surprise that respective governments of Azad Kashmir have very little or no interest in the freedom of the State of Jammu and Kashmir.

Text

A. **Matters within the purview of the Government of Pakistan.**

1. Defence (as modified under....).
2. Foreign policy of Azad Kashmir.
3. Negotiations with the United Nations Commission for India and Pakistan.
4. Publicity in foreign countries and in Pakistan.
5. Co-ordination and arrangement of relief and rehabilitation of refugees.

6. Co-ordination of publicity in connection with plebiscite.

7. All activities within Pakistan regarding Kashmir such as procurement of food, civil supplies running of refugee camps and medical aid.

8. All affairs of Gilgit-Ladakh under the control of Political Agent.

B. Matters within the purview of Azad Kashmir Government.

1. Policy with regard to administration of AK territory.

2. General supervision of administration in AK territory.

3. Publicity with regard to the activities of the Azad Kashmir Government and administration.

4. Advice to the honourable Minister without portfolio with regard to negotiations with United Nations Commission for India and Pakistan.

5. Development of economic resources of AK territory.

C. Matters within the purview of the Muslim Conference.

1. Publicity with regard to plebiscite in the AK territory.

2. Field work and publicity in the Indian occupied area of the State.

3. Organisation of political activities in the AK territory and the Indian occupied area of the State.

4. Preliminary arrangements in connection with the plebiscite.

5. Organisation for contesting the plebiscite.

6. Political work and publicity among the Kashmiri refugees in Pakistan.

7. Advise the honourable minister without Portfolio with regard to the negotiations with the United Nations Commission for India and Pakistan.

Retrieved from "http://en.wikisource.org/wiki_Karachi_Agreement"

Appendix-II

Legislative List of the State Council of "Azad Jammu and Kashmir" Third Schedule of the interim Constitution, 1974

1. Subject to the responsibilities of the Government of Pakistan under the UNCIP resolutions, nationality, citizenship and naturalization, migration from or into Azad Jammu and Kashmir, including in relation thereto the regulation of the movements in Azad Jammu and Kashmir of persons not domiciled in Azad Jammu and Kashmir.

2. Post and Telegraphs including Telephones wireless, Broadcasting and other forms of Communication; Post Office Saving Banks.

3. Public debts of the Council; including borrowing of money on the security of the Council Consolidated Fund.

4. Council public services and Council Public Service Commission.

5. Council Pensions, that is to say, pensions payable by the Council out of the Council Consolidated Fund.

6. Administrative courts for Council subjects.

7. Council agencies and institutions for the following purpose, that is to say, for research, for professional

or technical training, or for the promotion of special studies.

8. Nuclear energy, including

   (a) mineral resources necessary for the generation of nuclear energy;

   (b) the production of nuclear fuels and the generation and use of nuclear energy; and

   (c) ionizing radiations.

9. Aircraft and air navigation; the provision of aerodromes, regulations and organizations of air traffic of aerodromes.

10. Beacons and other provisions for safety of aircraft.

11. Carriage of passengers and goods by air.

12. Copyright, inventions, design, trade marks.

13. Opium only for export.

14. Banking, that is to say, the coordination with the Government of Pakistan of the conduct of banking business.

15. The law of insurance and the regulation of the conduct of insurance business.

16. Stock-exchange and future markets with objects and business not confined to Azad Jammu and Kashmir.

17. Corporation, that is to say, the incorporation, regulation and winding up of trading corporation including banking, insurance and financial corporations owned or controlled by Azad Jammu and Kashmir, or, co-operative societies and of corporations whether trading or not, with objects not confined to Azad Jammu and Kashmir, but not including universities.

18. Planning for economic coordination, including planning and coordination of scientific and technological research.

19. Highways, continuing beyond the territory of Azad Jammu and Kashmir, excluding roads declared by the Government of Pakistan to be of strategic importance.

20. Council surveys including geological surveys and Council meteorological oraganizations.

21. Works, lands and building vested in, or in the possession of, the Council for the purposes of the Council (not being military, naval or air force works, but, as regards property situated in Azad Jammu and Kashmir, subject always to law made by the Legislative Assembly, save in so far as law made by the Council otherwise provides).

22. Census.

23. Establishment of standards of weight and measures.

24. Extension of the powers and jurisdiction of memoirs of a police force belonging to Azad Jammu and Kashmir or any other province of Pakistan to any area in such province or Azad Jammu and Kashmir, but not so as to enable the police of Azad Jammu and Kashmir or such province to exercise powers and jurisdictions in such province or Azad Jammu and Kashmir with the consent of the Government of that province or Azad Jammu and Kashmir; extension of power jurisdiction of members of a police force belonging to the Azad Jammu and Kashmir or a Province of Pakistan to railway areas outside Azad Jammu and Kashmir or that province.

25. Election to the Council.

26. The salaries, allowances and privileges of the members of the Council and Advisors.

27. Railways.

28. Mineral oil and natural gas; liquids and substances declared by law made by the Council to be dangerously inflammable.

29. Removal of prisoners and accused persons from Azad Jammu and Kashmir to Pakistan or from Pakistan to Azad Jammu and Kashmir.

30. Measures to combat certain offences committed in connection with matters concerning the Council and the Government and the establishment of a police force for that purpose (or the extension to Azad Jammu and Kashmir of the jurisdiction of a police force established in Pakistan for the investigation of offences committed in connection with matters concerning the Government of Pakistan).

31. Prevention of extension from Azad Jammu and Kashmir to Pakistan or from Pakistan to Azad Jammu and Kashmir of infectious or contagious diseases or pests affecting men, animals and plants.

32. Population planning and social welfare.

33. Boilers.

34. Electricity.

35. Newspapers, books and printing presses.

36. State property.

37. Curriculum. Syllabus, planning, policy, centres of excellence and standards of education.

38. Sanctioning of cinematograph films for exhibition.

39. Tourism.

40. Duties of customs, including export duties.

41. Taxes on income other than agricultural income.

42. Taxes on corporations.

43. Taxes on capital value of the assets not including taxes on capital gains or immovable property.

44. Taxes and duties on the production capacity of any plant, machinery, undertaking, establishment or installation in lieu of the taxes and duties specified in

entries 42 and 43 or in lieu of either or both of them.

45. Terminal taxes on goods or passengers carried by railway or air, taxes on their fares and freights.

46. Fees in respect of any of the matters enumerated in this list but does not include fees taken in the court.

47. Jurisdiction and powers of all courts with respect to any of the matters enumerated in this list.

48. Offences against laws with respect to any of the matters enumerated in this list.

49. Inquiries and statistics for the purposes of any of the matters enumerated in this list.

50. Matters which under the Act are within the legislative competence or relate to the Council.

51. Matters incidental or ancillary to any of the matters enumerated in this list.

9

Economic Exploitation of Gilgit-Baltistan

Shafqat Inqalabi

The land which lies amidst towering mountains and contains eight of the world's highest mountain peaks apart from Mount Everest and Kanchanjunga, is traditionally called Gilgit-Baltistan. It has snow clad peaks, mighty glaciers second only to the North Pole and narrow lush green valleys "with heights varying from 3000 feet to 28,250 feet above sea level."[1] It covers an area of about 28,000 square miles. Nature has blessed this piece of earth, which was known as Brooshaal till the sixth century. Later it came to be known by the name of Bloristan and finally as Dardistan. In twentieth century the land was called Gilgit-Baltistan and Gilgit Agency. During 1970s, the Pakistani occupants in a clever move deliberately distorted the facts and with malafide intentions renamed it as the 'Northern Areas'.

At present Pakistani media and administration call it 'Northern Areas' of Pakistan, even though it is a serious violation of UN resolutions on Kashmir. Local residents prefer to call it as Balwaristan. This fulcrum of central Asia is a living paradise on earth and has abundance of natural resources but despite abundance of resources, the so-called 'Northern Areas' constitute the most backward areas in the entire South Asia and the region seems to have missed the development bus completely. The literacy rates in the region are at 14 per cent far below Pakistan's national average of 31 per cent and the literacy rate of women is abysmally low at 3.5 per cent. There is one doctor for every 6000 people and one hospital bed for 1500 people. Local people are extremely poor and live in some of the harshest environmental conditions of weather and terrain. In summers the mercury often rises above 40°C; whereas in the winters, it drops below -25°C. The basic facilities, such as electricity, drinking water and elementary healthcare are virtually non-existent. "Once autonomous and self-sufficient in food, the people in the Northern Areas are today dependent on the KKH for most of their needs including food. In recent years, a lethal mix of earthquakes, floods and political crises has rendered this crucial lifeline vulnerable, jeopardising the lives of over a million people."[2] The entire region does not have any kind of industry and over 85 per cent of the people live below the poverty line. People mostly depend on government offered jobs and join defence related institutions to earn their livelihood.

Tourism Potential

Before Pakistan went nuclear, tourism was the economic lifeline, but the explosions mixed with the aftermath of the 9/11 have almost dried up this avenue. God has blessed this paradise on earth by huge water resources, large variety of fruits, forests, beautiful lakes, rivers, springs, largest glaciers and minerals. Despite huge publicity only 4000 foreign tourists could be attracted for K2 Golden jubilee celebrations in 2004.[3] The resultant unemployment and lack of opportunities have "created an explosive situation" and have led to "widespread unrest and frustration" in the masses.[4]

However, despite the setbacks, it is still the most sought after tourist destination in entire Pakistan and areas under its occupation. According to official estimates some 80 per cent of foreign tourists coming to Pakistan, visit Balawaristan every year. The area however, does not derive any tangible benefits from the visits as it unfortunately has no local authority of its own, being a disputed area of former state of Jammu and Kashmir. On the other hand, the Pakistanis who have illegally occupied the region earn over rupees 4.5 billion from the tourists, who visit Balawaristan without paying anything to the local people. The area has numerous high peaks including the second highest peak in the world K2 (28,250 feet)[5], the foreign mountaineers, who visit Pakistan to scale these challenging peaks are charged rupees seven to eight million per team by the Pakistani government.

Mineral Resources

The region is rich in mineral resources and produces a number of precious metals and important radioactive material. Gilgit-Baltistan has huge reserves of gold and a number of gold mines exist in the region. Even before 1947 most of the vassal states used to pay the Maharaja of Jammu and Kashmir tribute in the form of gold dust. According to a joint report prepared by the Australian Agency for International Development (AUAID) and Pakistan Mineral Development Corporation (PMDC) in 1995, there are 1480 gold mines in this area, out of which 123 have ore where the gold content is many times higher than the world famous mines of South Africa. The gold content at South African gold mines is 20 to 31 parts per million (ppm), where as 123 gold mines of Balawaristan have a gold content of 112 to 238 ppm. During the study as many as 2380 stream sediment samples were analysed and they were discovered to have significant contents of silver, copper, lead, cobalt, zinc, nickel and bismuth besides gold.[6] Only 70 of these mines in Balawaristan are estimated to be worth 500 trillion dollars. The reserves of remaining 1410 gold mines are yet to be estimated. If the gold from these 70 gold mines was to be distributed among the 2 million people of Balawaristan the share of each person would be approximately rupees 1.25 million per year for next 100 years.

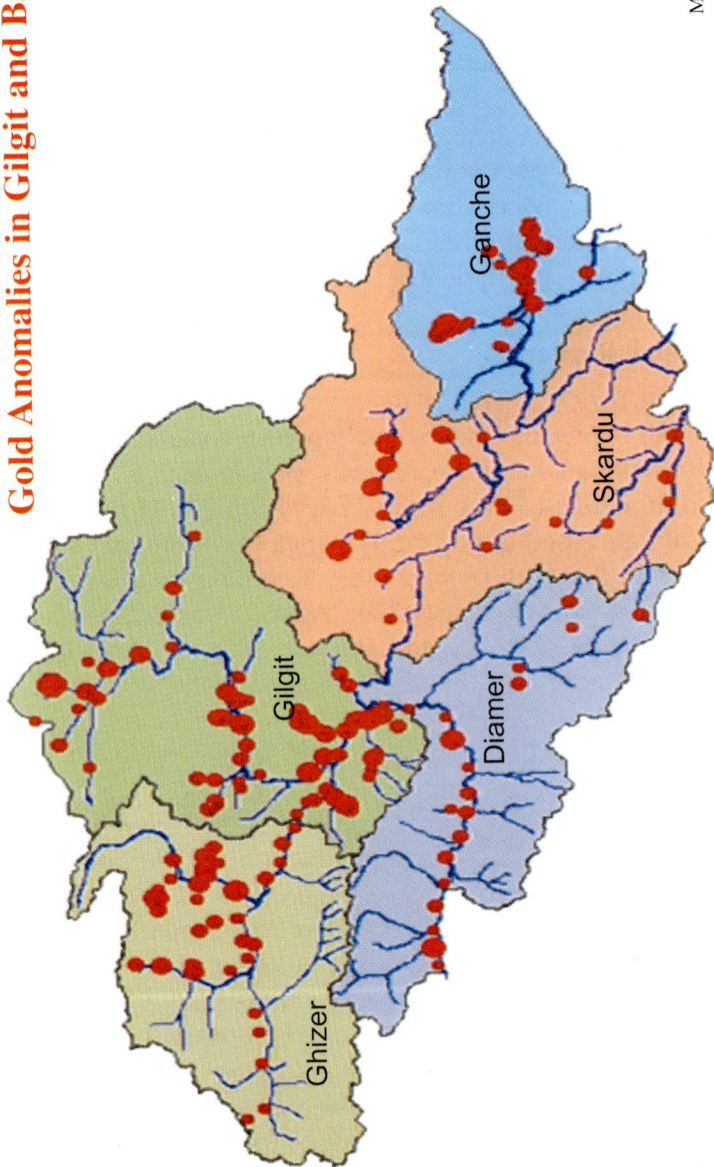
Gold Anomalies in Gilgit and Baltistan

Ganche

Skardu

Gilgit

Diamer

Ghizer

Map not to scale

The Pakistani government is planning to exploit these gold mines with the help of AUAID. According to the agreement, AUAID will get 54 per cent share, PMDC will get 23 per cent and the remaining 23 per cent will go to the Pakistani government, namely, the Ministry of Kashmir and Northern Areas Affairs (KANA) and the Pakistani administration based in Gilgit-Baltistan (Balawaristan). As far as the people of Balawaristan, who actually own the mines are concerned, they would get nothing. In addition, the region has mines of Uranium 238, Ruby, Emerald, Topaz, Quartz, Iron, Marble, Sulphur, Alum and Oil.

Water Resources

Despite being a rain deficit region, the region has enormous water resources as almost all peaks are covered with heavy snow in winter. The snow has resulted in a large number of glaciers in the region. Water flows in summer due to melting of mighty glaciers. Other water sources are the beautiful natural lakes, flowing into rivers and giving birth to the famous Indus River, which irrigates Pakistan. These mighty glaciers and streams which are tributaries of river Indus destroy thousands of acres of fertile land in Balawaristan every year but Pakistan gives rupees 6.5 billion to the North West Frontier Province (NWFP) as royalty on the pretext of Tarbela Dam, but nothing is paid to the resource owners i.e. the people of Balawaristan. "Less than ten per cent of the hydroelectric potential of the region has been tapped for local use."[7] This especially is ironic as Pakistan intends to build mega dams at Skardu and Bhasha which will inundate millions of acres of populated fertile land to provide cheap electricity to the rest of Pakistan.

Unfortunately Bhasha Dam has been so planned that the royalty from the Dam will go to NWFP as Article 161 (2) of the Pakistani constitution stipulates that the royalty and the bulk of the net profits earned from a hydroelectric station shall go to the province where the station is situated. The Bhasha Village, which will house only one per cent of the dam, is shown to be in the NWFP; hence earnings from the dam will mostly go to the NWFP even though the dam "would inundate 32 villages of Diamer District" of Gilgit and Baltistan, with a combined population of 26,000, and thousands of canals of agricultural land. "More than 125 kilometres of the Karakoram Highway will be submerged in water because of the dam." The people of the Gilgit and Baltistan feel "it is unfair for their land to be used to build a water reservoir" that would benefit Pakistan when their own territorial status has not been decided. In the absence of a constitutional status, the people of Gilgit and Baltistan are apprehensive if they would get any royalty from the dam.[8]

Although the Pakistani government has recently given assurances about sharing of royalty, it has failed to assuage the hurt sentiments of the locals, who insist that the entire royalty must come to them. People have also demanded that royalty "paid to NWFP for the Tarbela Dam since its commissioning to the tune of over Rs 20 billion be instead spent on the economic development" of Gilgit and Baltistan as the dam is actually located in Gilgit and Baltistan.[9] Many people in the Gilgit and Baltistan "complain that hydro-electric, tourism, mineral, and trade revenues of the region are being drained away to the federal coffers and used by other provinces", which in their view is nothing but exploitation.[10] They have accordingly been demanding fair returns on the natural resources of the region being used.[11]

Other Natural Resources

There are thick forests in the Dardistan Province of Balawaristan, which cover almost 11,000 hectares of the land. These forests yield to the government of Pakistan a revenue of more than rupees 1.5 billion by way of timber, even after misappropriation by the corrupt Pakistani officials. On the other hand, the local people who are the actual owners are paid a meagre amount as royalty and are also denied the traditional usage of forest products. The region also abounds with a large number of exotic wild animals and birds, which are rare in other parts of the world. Markhors (ibex) Markopolo sheep, snow tigers, leopards, oxen, snow bears, eagles, vultures, kites, red leg patridges, tohchons, choughs, pygmies and so many birds of prey and other birds are found in this paradise of earth. The estimated income to the Pakistani State from wildlife is approximately rupees one billion. Pakistan's military and civil officers deputed in Balawaristan are known to hunt these rare animals and birds by helicopter gunships and smuggle some exotic birds to Arab Sheikhs to earn petro dollars.

The region has numerous freshwater bodies and as this paradise has clean and mineral water everywhere in large quantity, the breeding of fish is much higher than in other parts of the world. The water bodies in the region are home to rare species of tout fish. The fisheries contribute approximately rupees ten million annually to the Pakistani exchequer, but the irresponsible Pakistani Military and Civil officers, often out of greed, use detonators to blast the whole area, where the fish are available, as a result, this precious resource is fast becoming extinct and is causing resentment amongst locals, who feel that they are being deprived of this precious gift of God.

Other Sources of Revenue

Gilgit and Baltistan link Pakistan to China. Karakoram Highway (KKH) is the road link between Pakistan and China. The 857 kilometer long KKH was constructed without paying a single penny to the local people and on the other hand, it led to the ceding of 2500 square miles of Shaksgam Valley an area of the former State of Hunza to China, illegally, apparently to get Chinese assistance to build this highway. China wants to link up Gwadar to Gilgit and has constructed a dry port at Sust 140 km North of Gilgit, which was inaugurated by General Musharraf on July 4, 2006.[12] It now intends to expand and realign the Karakoram Highway which will enable it to access the port to facilitate exports from Chinese factories located in north-western China. Pakistan earns billions of dollars from the highway. Besides, military equipment from China comes via Karakoram Highway, but no royalty is paid to the local people. Approximately a revenue of rupees three billion annually is earned by the Pakistani State by way of customs duty received at Sust Custom check post in Hunza, even though Pakistan has no right to collect taxes from this disputed land.

Despite the region being disputed and Pakistan having no right to collect any tax from the region, besides customs duty earned from Sust Customs, it collects approximately rupees 2.7 Billion as indirect taxes from the goods imported to this region from Pakistani markets. Of these rupees 200 to 300 million are acquired by way of customs duty from the Khunjrab border of disputed region of Balwaristan and are deposited with Pakistani exchequer, while rupees 2.30 billion go into the pockets of rulers through Pakistan's customs staff. In addition, the direct taxes have been imposed on the people living in this disputed and unconstitutional land.

Conclusion

The Northern Areas has no university[13] and no professional colleges. It has only 12 high schools and two regional colleges with no post-graduate facilities. Lack of education has practically closed all avenues of government jobs, thus negating their upliftment. This has led to the demand for reservation in Indian educational institutions. There are no daily newspapers and no radio or TV stations. The local people draw their subsistence from tourism, which has declined considerably and by joining the Northern Light Infantry, recruitment in which has now been reduced considerably. Government service is another means of livelihood, but the natives who manage to join service are paid 25 per cent less than non-native entrants from the Punjab province. Funds earmarked for developmental schemes often lapse. The mainstay of the economy in this area is essentially agriculture, but like every feudal society, most of the land is held by a privileged few and the rest continue to live in sub-human conditions. According to an editorial in the *Dawn*, the government claims that it has enhanced the 'Northern Areas' development funds by 183 per cent in the past five years but there has been hardly anything to show for all this. Gilgit and Baltistan "continue to remain under-developed and impoverished, despite the 740 development schemes reportedly underway" in the region.[14] Frustration arising from unemployment and discrimination is acting as catalyst for people to come out on the streets. As the region has been kept outside the jurisdiction of courts, the people receive no redress. An indifferent bureaucracy, and political leadership, and an oppressive army, have all put Gilgit and Baltistan on a turbulent course, which may not be possible to change.

Despite being resource rich region, the resources are being exploited by Pakistanis, who are in illegal occupation of this region, without any benefit accruing to the local population. Pakistan has spared no repression against occupied Balawaristan and has kept the region deprived of all fundamental, democratic and political rights. It has neither granted the 'right to vote' to two million people nor have they been granted, the due role according to the UNCIP resolution. This region is legally and internationally disputed and cannot be included in the Pakistani constitution. It is neither a tribal area of Pakistan nor a part of any province. However, all laws are enforced with immediate effect in this region for repression and exploitation. Moreover, Pakistan as an aggressor and unjust country has imposed all taxes, on the impoverished people of this region who are already living in abject poverty and are already the victim of the worst kind of tyrannies in the world.

Notes

1 Syed Abdul Quddus, *The North-West Frontier of Pakistan.* Karachi: Royal Book Company, 1990, p. 242.

2 M. Ismail Khan, "Avoiding the Highway of Death", *The International News*, Internet Edition, May 5, 2005.

3 Farman Ali, "Gilgit-Baltistan residents request border crossings at Skardu", *The Herald*, April 2005, p. 50.

4 Ershad Mahmud. "Challenges Before the New Government in NAs", *The International News*, Internet Edition, December 11, 2004.

5 Syed Abdul Quddus, n.1, p. 242.

6 Pakistan Mineral Development Corporation Website http://www.pmdc.gov.pk/pmdc-final/invest.htm#2 (Accessed on October 12, 2006).

7 Aabha Dixit, "Ethnicity and Human Rights" in Jasjit Singh (ed), *Pakistan Occupied Kashmir: Under The Jackboot*, New Delhi: Siddhi Books, 1995, pp. 197-198.

8 Ibrahim Shahid, "Basha Dam may leave Northern Areas high and dry", from *Daily Times* Website http://www.dailytimes.com.pk/default.asp? page = 2006% 5C02% 5C21% 5Cstory_21-2-2006_pg7_36 (Accessed on March 1, 2006).

9 Aabha Dixit, n.7, p. 204.

10 M Ismail Khan, "Kashmir's Scapegoats", *The International News*, Internet Edition, June 25, 2005.

11 Aabha Dixit, n.7, p. 204.

12 Safdar Khan, "Karakoram Highway's Gwadar link likely", *Dawn*, Karachi, July 5, 2006.

13 Karakoram International University was established in 2005 but is plagued by acute shortage of staff and requisite infrastructure.

14 "Bringing peace to Gilgit", Editorial, *Dawn*, Karachi, January 3, 2006.

10

The Indus, POK and the Peace Process: Building on the Foundations of the Indus Water Treaty

B.G.Verghese

The Indus Water Treaty must rank among the triumphs of the United Nations system since it was signed in 1960. It has worked remarkably well in keeping the peace, with the onus of performance falling almost entirely on India as the upper riparian, despite constant nit-picking by Pakistan. Islamabad has, especially latterly, cranked up political "disputes" on the Indus by periodically raising objections to India's Sallal and Baglihar projects on the Chenab and Tulbul and Kishenganga projects on the Jhelum system.

Having taken a slow 180 degree turn, first tactical and then more strategic, on the ideological or territorial ("unfinished business of Pakistan") aspect of the J&K question after 9/11, Pakistan has been anxious to demonstrate that it has not relented on the "core" issue. Meanwhile, growing water stress and inter-provincial water rivalries have increasingly become part of the political discourse. Hence the charge that India is threatening its "lifeline" by not merely misappropriatingly Indus waters in violation of the Treaty but, in doing so, it is developing strategic capability to hurt Pakistan by drying up these rivers or causing floods!

The "lifeline" issue was first raised when East Punjab cut off supplies to the Central Bari Doab (CBD) and Dipalpur Canals on April 1, 1948, a day after the expiry of the Standstill Agreement on canal waters signed in December 1947. These supplies amounted to six per cent of the canal flows to Pakistan and did not affect the far larger flows serving dozens of its other canals. Supplies to the CBD and Dipalpur Canals were restored on April 30 and the new agreement was ratified by India and Pakistan on May 4, 1948. Nehru was furious with the East Punjab for acting unilaterally in the first place. Chaudhry Muhammad Ali, Pakistan's Secretary-General, wrote in *The Emergence of Pakistan* that while East Punjab showed "Machiavellian duplicity", West Punjab displayed "neglect of duty, complacency and lack of common prudence" in failing to renew the original standstill agreement in time.[1]

The Canal Water dispute triggered complex negotiations culminating in the Indus Water Treaty, brokered by the World Bank. The 168 Million Acre Feet (MAF) average annual flow of the Indus was divided in the ratio of 80:20, with Pakistan getting the lion's share in the form of the entire flow of the three Western Rivers (the Indus, Jhelum and Chenab) plus the Kabul, barring some limited Indian uses in J&K. India was, in turn, allocated the entire water of the three smaller Eastern Rivers (Ravi, Beas and Sutlej), less some minor uses for Pakistan from the Ravi.

Pakistan received generous assistance from a World Bank-led consortium and India was called upon to pay 62 million pound sterling to Pakistan towards replacement works to be built by it within a transitional period of 10 years ending in 1970. With this settlement, Pakistan was able to develop a completely independent irrigation system with storages at Tarbela (Indus) and Mangla (Jhelum), while India was able to redesign and complete Bhakra and later build the Pong and Thein Dams (on the Beas and Ravi) and other storages. Assurance of these waters was an important factor making for the Green Revolution that followed.

Subsequently, in all these 46 years since 1960, despite wars, proxy-war and cross-border terrorism and alarms and excursions of every kind, when everything else failed, the Indus Commissioners continued to meet and the Indus Treaty worked. The "lifeline" problem should demonstrably have been laid to rest.

India's rights on the three Western rivers are clearly and specifically set out in the 1960 Treaty. All existing irrigation, hydroelectric (hydel) flood moderation and navigational uses in J&K were protected. Over and beyond that, India was permitted to develop additional irrigation of 1.34 million acres in J&K, against which only 642,477 acres has been achieved so far, leaving a balance of over half a million acres. Further, India is allowed 3.60 MAF of storage (0.40 MAF on the Indus, 1.50 MAF on the Jhelum and 1.70 MAF on the Chenab). This in turn has been categorized sector-wise: 2.85 MAF for conservation storage (divided into 1.25 MAF for "general storage" and 1.60 MAF for "power storage") and an additional 0.75 MAF for "flood storage". These have been further classified under the headings of main rivers and tributaries. The fact is that till today, India is well below the permissible limits in every sector and category of usage and has built practically no "storages" (as opposed to run-of-the-river "pondages").

The Treaty binds India to inform or consult Pakistan on planned withdrawals and works on the Western rivers and to ensure no harm or derogation of its water rights. There have been 27 occasions when such information has been passed or consultations organised and the record shows that Pakistan has raised objections in virtually all cases, even with regard to mini/micro hydro plants with miniscule pondages in respect of which "adverse comments" have been passed and such projects have been dropped subsequently if they generated electricity below 1 MW capacity. The objections have generally been qualitative ("Treaty violation") without quantification and substantiation. In other words, though dressed up as design or engineering objections or queries, the objective has been political and the motivation to delay, if not deny, progress that primarily benefits J&K.

This, and admittedly some of India's own internal delays, has irked opinion in J&K, which feels that the State has had to bear the burden of the Indus Treaty with the benefits flowing to Punjab, Haryana, Rajasthan, Delhi and others. Abrogation of the Treaty has sometimes been advocated. This is a mistaken view as J&K and India as a whole have yet to utilise their full entitlement. Moreover, talk of abrogating the Treaty would gratuitously revive and breathe life into Pakistan's "lifeline" argument.

India has complete entitlement to the entire waters of the Sutlej, Beas and Ravi, leaving Pakistan with no rights on them excepting for no more than irrigating 100 acres of land from the Basantar, a tributary of the Ravi. Despite this, India released as much as 4.85 MAF (mostly flood waters) down the Sutlej and Ravi into Pakistan on an average between 1990 and 2002. This has since reduced to about 3 MAF after the completion of the Thein dam on the Ravi, with the balance still escaping on account of the dispute over the Sutlej-Yamuna Link and the fact that the final phase of the Indira Gandhi (Rajasthan) Canal is yet to be completed.

It is against this statement of water accounts under the Treaty, that one should view Pakistan's objections to the Baglihar and Kishenganga projects.

Baglihar is a run-of-the-river peaking project on the Chenab, above the Salal Dam, and over 110 km from the Pakistan border. It has an installed capacity of 450 MW and a live pondage of 37.5 million cubic metres (mcm) of water (or 46,570 acre-feet), the balance of the gross 396 mcm pondage being dead storage. In accordance with the Treaty, the volume of water received in the pond over each seven-day period shall be returned to the river below the dam within the same week, each 24-hour return flow ranging between a minimum of 30 per cent and maximum of 130 per cent of the inflow received within that same 24-hour period. Baglihar should start generating by 2007.

With basically no more than the addition of more turbines and some other minor works, Baglihar-II will generate another 450 MW for three or four monsoon months.

Pakistan was informed as far back as 1992 that India planned to go ahead with Baglihar. Work commenced in 2000 on the basis of 25-year flow data that was communicated to and never challenged by Islamabad. The minimum average flow of the Chenab at Baglihar in January is 125 cumecs (4375 cusecs) and the dam is designed to pass a maximum flood of 12,600 cumecs . It is only in the last couple of years that objections were being pressed and then specified in January 2005. The six objections raised by Pakistan related to pondage, gated spillways, under-sluices and the level of the intake channel. But the punch line was that the dam would be able to store/release a quantum of water sufficient to flood Pakistan or dry up the river for several days.

India has argued that these fears are fanciful as all the parameters conform to the Treaty and flooding or drying up of the river (and Pakistan's canal anti-tank ditches) is simply not possible. The fallacy lies in adding dead storage to live pondage and assuming malafide intent that would primarily, and first, adversely affect the Indian villages along the Chenab valley and the Salal Dam. Indeed, Pakistan is so far away that any flood water would dissipate before they reached the border.

The same argument of flooding or drying up the river has been used to stymie other Indian proposals, be it Salal, Uri or Dul Hasti. In short, Pakistan's argument appears to be that every dam can be used as a strategic weapon of war. This is perverse reasoning.

Indian experts are of the view that if another couple of rounds of talks had been held after Pakistan quantified its objections, complete convergence could have been reached.

Unfortunately, Pakistan insisted on resorting to the difference-dispute settlement mechanism under the Treaty. The Neutral Expert since appointed can either give a finding that will be binding or certify a "dispute" which either party may then refer to arbitration as provided. Pakistan's condition for continuing talks on Baglihar and Kishenganga (after a July 2005 deadline) was that construction must stop. The Treaty does not provide for such stoppage and India accordingly declined to do so, especially in view of the fact that it agreed to a temporary stoppage of work on the Tulbul Project, which stands unresolved for 17 years.

The Jhelum was traditionally used for navigation and floating timber down to Sopore and Baramulla, but the river has silted. The Tulbul Project was accordingly designed to retard the Jhelum flood within the natural confines of the Wular Lake through which the river passes. Instead of emptying swiftly with the receding flood, a control structure at the Lake's exit would have permitted steady releases of this natural pondage of some 300,000 acre feet of water through the lean months from October to May. This would have reduced silt flows downstream to the benefit of both the Uri and Mangla projects in India and Pakistan by augmenting their power output. However, Pakistan argues that Tulbul would be a storage dam and is, therefore, barred by the Treaty. India looks on it as no more than a flood retardation device. Thanks to Pakistan, Tulbul remains in limbo.

As regards to Kishenganga, or the Neelum as this tributary of the Jhelum is known in Pakistan, after rising near Gurez, the river flows through J&K and then crosses the LoC to enter POK before falling into the Jhelum near Muzaffarabad. The original Indian Project envisaged a 75 m high concrete dam on the Kishenganga at Gurez at an altitude of about 8000 feet. It was to store 140,000 MAF of water and divert flows southwards through a 23 km tunnel into a Jhelum tributary, the Madmati Nala that flows into the Wular Lake through which the Jhelum runs. The proposed water diversion was quite small but, given a high head of about 600 m, an installed capacity of 330 MW was planned. The quantum of displacement and environmental impacts, however, raised sensitive issues that would have had to be internally addressed.

An incidental advantage of the Kishenganga diversion was that it would flush the Wulur Lake and help rejuvenate this important water body.

India had communicated its intention of going ahead with the Kishenganga project in June 1992 and Pakistan responded soon after, listing three objections. The first was that inter-tributary diversions are barred and that waters drawn from a given river must be returned to that same river. The second was that existing Pakistani uses must be protected and India's Kishenganga Project would deprive it of 27 per cent of the river's natural flows, thereby doing injury to its "existing" 133,000 ha of irrigation in the Neelum Valley and a 900 MW Neelum-Jhelum hydel station on which construction had supposedly commenced at Nowshera. The third objection related to certain design features of the dam.

The Indian response was that the Indus Water Treaty is unambiguous. Section 15(3) of Part 3 (regarding new run-of-river plants) of Annexure D, pertaining to "Generation of hydro-electric power by India on the Western Rivers", reads as follows: "Where a plant is located on a tributary of the Jhelum on which Pakistan has an agricultural use or hydro-electric use, the water released below the plant may be delivered, if necessary, into another tributary but only to the extent that the then existing agricultural use or hydro-electric use by Pakistan on the former tributary would not be adversely affected." A plain reading of this would suggest that inter-tributary diversions in the Jhelum basin are permitted and that only "the then existing" agricultural and hydro-electric uses shall be protected.

The next question is what the phrase "the then existing" uses implies? Pakistan has to substantiate and not merely assert

133,000 ha of irrigation. Hard evidence on this was not forthcoming. And what is the stage of construction or operation of the Nowshera hydro-electric plant and what are its specifications? A planned use would be a future use not an existing use. Would the same argument apply to a planned diversion by India on which work has recently commenced? In any event, the Neelum catchment below the Kishenganga dam receives several influent flows that make the discharge at Nowshera many times larger than that the mean flows at Gurez. Both sides had agreed to visit each other's Kishenganga/Neelum sites before the end-July 2005, the deadline Pakistan initially set, before it formally referred this "difference" to a Neutral Expert. The only extension it was willing to consider was if India agreed to halt construction on the Kishenganga project. India declined to do this knowing from past experience that delay means denial.

However, India subsequently decided in April 2005 to redesign the Kishenganga scheme as a run-of-river rather than as a storage project. This will save submergence in the Gurez Valley on the Indian side of the LoC and has been proposed solely in response to the local concerns. With this, little of the original "difference" remains. What the October 2005 earthquake in POK has done to Pakistan's Neelum-Jhelum irrigation and hydro-power projects is not known. The Indus Commissioners at their last meeting in Lahore from May 10 to May 12, 2006, decided on further meetings and site inspections. This meeting is yet to take place. It has throughout been India's position that it has scrupulously abided by the Indus Water Treaty and should any genuine problem be pointed out by Pakistan, it would be prepared to make suitable modifications. This assurance has once again been reiterated by Dr Manmohan Singh.

India will need to build storages to utilise the irrigation potential permitted under the Indus Water Treaty. J&K also has considerable hydel potential that should be exploited for the benefit of the State and the country as a whole. Schemes like Sewa (120 MW), Sawalkote (600 MW), Burser (1029 MW) and Pakaldul (1000 MW), both on a Chenab tributary, Kirthai I and II (600 MW), Parnai, (37.5 MW, on the Poonch river), Ujh (96 MW, on a Ravi tributary) and several smaller and mini/micro schemes are on the anvil in the State and Central sectors. These will stimulate development and employment in J&K and help open up remote areas by providing connectivity.

A 1987 river resource reassessment by the CEA placed J&K's identified unutilised hydro potential at 14,146 MW (installed capacity) — 17 per cent of this on the Indus spread over a number of small schemes, 19 per cent on the Jhelum, and over 63 per cent on the Chenab (some of this in Himachal).

The Indus Commission is required to submit an annual report to the two Governments in June each year and may undertake at the request of either Commissioner a tour of inspection of such works or sites as may be considered necessary by him for ascertaining the facts connected with those works or sites. This is in addition to the duty enjoined on the Commission to undertake "a general tour of inspection" every five years to ascertain facts pertaining to the Rivers and works thereon. It would be in the fitness of things that this right is exercised as developments are taking place or planned or under discussion in the POK and Pakistan that require closer understanding and public airing.

Pakistan has an entitlement of 135 MAF of the total water of the Indus system. Inter-provincial discords have come in the way of their fuller utilisation through further storages. The Kalabagh dam (gross storage of 7.9 MAF) has been stalled for years by NWFP and Sind. A run-of-the-river Ghazi Barotha hydel project came on stream in June 2004, but the Bhasha-Diamer storage dam in Gilgit-Baltistan (Northern Areas) despite running into opposition at the feasibility stage has nevertheless been cleared for construction in February 2006. The dam will inundated large areas in POK to provide electricity to Pakistan.

The Mangla dam on the Jhelum was completed as part of the transition works under the Indus Water Treaty. It also flooded vast areas in POK and displaced large number of families. It had a gross storage of 4.5 MAF but has suffered heavy siltation that has reduced its effective capacity. Pakistan, accordingly, contracted the China International Water and Electric Corporation in June 2004 to raise the height of the dam by 30 feet to store an additional 2.88 MAF of water and yield some 12 per cent more energy. The project will displace 44,000 persons. Accordingly 15,780 acres of land is being acquired for a new resettlement city. A bridge across the Jhelum and an 18 km Mirpur by-pass are also part of the compensation package. The project is due to be completed by September 2007.

Failure to pay adequate compensation and provide alternative connectivity for villagers displaced and divided by the Mangla lake in the 1960s led to a mass exodus of marginalized Mirpuris to the UK. Divided families on the Indian side must now hope that the resettlement and compensation package this time around does not lead to a further exodus.

Pakistan's water worries should concern India. Both sides share the Indus and it is only if they join hands that its potential can be optimised with sustainability to combat the common peril of climate change. Three separate reports submitted to the Pakistan Government by parliamentary, technical and international expert committees set out the country's water prospects. Sharp inter-provincial differences, largely revolving around Punjab's dominance, and the need to accommodate Afghanistan's demands on the Kabul River have shaped the discourse.

Strangely, both sides have ignored the idea of maximising mutual benefit through further Indo-Pakistan cooperation under the Indus Water Treaty. Hopefully, the impending report of the Neutral Expert on India's Baglihar project on the Chenab will, hopefully, signal a change from confrontation to cooperation as the futility of beggar-my-neighbour policies will soon become apparent.

Pakistan has a cultivated area of 40 million acres and an irrigable potential of 38.86 m acres. Pakistan's (West Pakistan's) population was 34 m in 1951, but had risen to 146 m by 2003 and is likely to touch 221 m by 2025. This will mean a per capita water availability of 1200 cu m by 2010 and 800 cu m by 2025. Like India, Pakistan is a wasteful water user and has to improve use efficiency. Canal modernisation, including lining and a telemetry system, are under way.

Pakistan currently diverts 117.35 MAF from the Indus, two-thirds of this during the kharif season. Another 8 MAF is used for drinking, sanitation and industrial purposes. A further average daily flow of 5000 cusecs (10 MAF) is required to escape to the sea below the Kotri barrage for the purpose of fisheries, coastal and delta management, preservation of mangroves and to prevent saltwater intrusion. The entire 33 MAF flow of the three Eastern Rivers has been allocated to India under the Indus Treaty, but apart from regenerated supplies, about 3 MAF still flows into Pakistan. Additionally, while India is entitled to irrigate 1.34 m acres of land in J&K from the three Western rivers, it has still to irrigate some 0.52 m acres and Pakistan estimates it will never use more than 2 MAF under this entitlement.

Currently Pakistan uses almost 90-95 per cent of Kabul waters. However, Afghanistan has started on the road to development and has arid areas to irrigate. A UNESCO-Iran study on possible Afghan uses is under way; but Pakistan believes that this requirement will not exceed 0.50 MAF.

Pakistan has no storage sites on the Chenab and only one site on the Jhelum, at Mangla just within POK. It has lost 30 per cent of overall storage capacity at Mangla, Tarbela and Chasma (the latter two on the Indus) on account of sedimentation. It is raising Mangla by 30 feet to store an additional 2.9 MAF and is desperately looking for other sites on the Indus. Kalabagh, below Tarbela, marks the lowest possible storage site (6.1 MAF, 3600 MW). But this dam is strongly opposed by NWFP and Sind. The Federal Government has recently approved the Bhasha-Diamer dam, near Chilas in Gilgit-Baltistan, 200 km upstream of Tarbela (7.34 MAF, 4500 MW, $6.7 bn as of 2002). NWFP supports Bhasha-Diamer but Pakistan feels that Bhasha-Diamer and Kalabagh should go together and can be completed by 2011-2014.

The Bhasha-Diamer project entails widening and upgrading the Karakoram Highway from Manshera to Chilas, itself a considerable undertaking. A dam as high as 905 feet appears problematic to some who advocate phased construction, going up to 600 feet in the first instance. Bhasha-Diamer lies beyond the arc of the monsoon and will, therefore, be entirely snow-fed like the proposed mega Katzarah dam (35,000 MAF, 15,000 MW), near Skardu, or the more modest Skardu dam alternative (8000-15,000 MAF, 4000 MW). The two latter dams would require even more elaborate highway improvements over a longer lead and entail high transmission costs over a bleak landscape to distant load centres.

The 'Northern Areas' was also insistent that the Bhasha dam be renamed as the Diamer-Bhasha Project for inclusion of Diamer in the very name would signify ownership and consequent benefits in terms of royalty, resettlement and compensation that the Mirpuris lost out in Mangla in the 1960s. This has been conceded and the official name of the project now stands amended to Diamer-Bhasha.

All the three dams, and even the proposed Kalabagh dam, would only fill in years of high flood, being essentially carryover dams to hold such "surplus storage". The Katzarah dam would submerge much of the Skardu bowl, the best of Balti civilisation and Pakistan's strategic communications. It has accordingly attracted considerable opposition even at the conceptual stage. According to the *Jang* newspaper and its English stable-mate,

The News, the 35 MAF Skardu Dam reservoir is likely to submerge the entire Skardu bowl and Shigar Valley leading up to K2, displacing a population of around 300,000 souls.[2] The hydro-electric potential of the site is also reportedly enormous. The project's driving force, Fatehullah Khan, former Chairman of the Indus River System Authority (IRSA), and the chair of WAPDA's Technical Committee on Water Resources, believe that the Katzarah project could be more than a substitute for the Kalabagh and Diamer-Bhasha dams and an answer to Pakistan's long-term water requirements. Sind also favours this option as Pakistan's carryover solution to wide annual flow variations, capturing 84 per cent of the available "storable surplus" in the system. Fatehullah Khan is said to be of the view that a detailed project report will be ready by 2009; work can commence by 2015 and be completed in eight years.

However, the Katzarah dam will all but drown and obliterate the finest in Balti culture and heritage and displace possibly half of the Balti population in Gilgit-Baltistan. This cannot be a good news for their cousins, the Indian Baltis in Kargil district, either. The Balwaristan nationalists too are up in arms and so are Pakistani conservationists and even sections of the security community who say that the project would submerge Pakistan's strategic roads, airfields and military supply lines in the region.

The Katzarah dam, as presently designed, may never move beyond the drawing board. But India should want to know more about such projects in POK, and could seek the necessary information and visit sites if necessary to ascertain the facts and assess the situation. Where would the estimated 300,000 Baltis go? Such questions need to be asked and answered, whether through the Indus Water Treaty mechanism or otherwise. There has already been much demographic change in the politically closed Gilgit and Baltistan to the detriment of the local Shia, Ismaili and Sufi communities.

Several run-of-river hydel sites are available in the upper Indus watershed and a substantial dam at Ghazi Barotha on the Indus was commissioned some years ago. But the only other storage sites of any significance are at Yogo on the Shyok and Akhori, on an "off-channel" taken from the Tarbela lake.

Cooperation with India in developing an Indus-II on the foundations of the 1960 Indus Water Treaty would probably yield Pakistan better and surer dividends, at less cost and sooner than its own futuristic proposals. India too would stand to benefit as it could then jointly survey sites with Pakistan for potential storages on the upper Indus in Ladakh and investigate the possibility of building or augmenting storages on the Chenab and Jhelum that are currently barred by the Indus Treaty beyond stipulated limits. The surplus waters of the Ravi and the other two Eastern Rivers that India cannot utilise could perhaps also be harnessed through joint cooperation, which could extend to developing the potential of the Indus system in the POK, on Pakistan's side of the LoC.

Exploration of this idea, could add a most useful and creative dimension to the current Indo-Pakistan peace process in J&K, covering land use, sediment control, agriculture, forestry, hydro energy, transmission and eco-tourism on both sides. This would make the J&K border "irrelevant", help build trans-border institutions across it and yield a huge peace dividend with manifold benefits to all the people of J&K.

This is a more rational way for Pakistan to seek water security. Happily it finds mention in the Indus Water Treaty itself. Article VII on future cooperation points to a "common interest in the optimum development of the Rivers" and calls upon both sides "to cooperate, by mutual consent, to the fullest possible extent ....in undertaking engineering works in the Rivers". The 1960 Treaty was a case of crisis management, conflict resolution arrangement that divided the waters so that immediate problems could be set aside and development plans could move forward. It has served that purpose admirably well. But it leaves behind a possibly large untapped potential in the upper catchments of the three Western Rivers that are allocated to Pakistan, barring certain uses to India, but which are under Indian control.

Article XII of the Indus Water Treaty provides that its provisions "may from time to time be modified by a duly ratified Treaty concluded for that purpose between the two Governments". Thus an Indus-II could be structured on the foundations of Indus-I. When the original treaty was being negotiated, India suggested a 2.5 MAF storage on the Chenab at Dhiangarh with a tunnel at Mahru to divert waters to the Ravi and Beas for delivery to Pakistan below Ferozepur in lieu of some other replacement works.

That was totally unacceptable to Pakistan at that time. Would it still be feasible and acceptable to Pakistan and India today were it to offer promise of adding to net water availability on both sides? The Chenab could perhaps also store more water in its upper reaches while the Indus has not really been surveyed from the point of view of storage. There may be little or nothing there. Do we know for certain?

The potential of the entire Indus system needs to be thoroughly surveyed and could thereafter, where it is sustainable, be harnessed through joint investment, construction, management and control. Pakistan cannot continue to deny India its limited entitlement in the Western rivers and also freeze all further development if it wants to grasp what could be a far larger prize by way of additional storage, flood moderation and hydro-power which both could share. India too could benefit from cooperative drainage arrangements in the middle and lower Indus basins. Were this to happen, Pakistan would not have to think of controversial schemes such as the Katrzarah dam that would spell doom for a proud civilization.

That both sides could benefit from Indus-II is certain. What is not known for sure is the quantum of that benefits and the costs involved. It is this that needs to be investigated, explored and conceptualized in the context of emerging hydrological uncertainties. With climate change, glaciers are in retreat both in the Karakoram—one of the most glaciated regions in the world that has the largest glaciers outside Antarctica—as well as on the Tibetan Plateau, from where the Indus and Sutlej originate. The Plateau is underlain by "tjale" or permafrost that shows signs of thawing. This suggests that enhanced glacier melt and thawing permafrost could increase flows in the Indus basin for some decades before declining sharply over the ensuing decades as the body of ice shrinks. This may be accompanied by shifts in rainfall patterns with the possibility of episodic bursts of precipitation in some areas. The uncertainty underlines the need for maximizing conservation storage within the limits of prudence and sustainability. The warning signals are there. A consultancy study for the World Bank by Wallingford of the UK, suggests that climate change and glacier melt could reduce Indus flows at Skardu by as much as 30 per cent within the next 30-40 years.

Climate change will not respect boundaries and both Pakistan and North West India, as wards of the Indus, therefore have a common interest in concerted action to study glacial behaviour and insure against future hazard from diminished glacial melt and stream flows combined with possibly more, though erratic, rainfall.

Dr Manmohan Singh has stated that that J&K's boundaries cannot be redrawn but soft borders can render them increasingly irrelevant. President Musharraf goes along with this, with the rider that the LoC as a permanent boundary cannot be a final and lasting solution by itself. The challenge is to find a solution within these three parameters.

At his meeting with the Editors' Guild of India on April 18, 2005, President Musharraf was asked if he would be ready to explore Indus-II as part of the answer to his conundrum. He replied in the affirmative, provided confidence was first assured on Indus-I. Soft borders, trade, tourism and management of Indus-II could, with other blossoming relationships, create cross-border mechanisms in J&K that foster interlocking jurisdictions on both sides of the LoC without derogation of the existing twin *de facto* sovereignties. Indus-II could, therefore, be fed into the current peace process as a means both of defusing current political strains over Indus-I and insuring against climate change. Moreover, it could reinforce the basis for a lasting solution to the J&K question by helping transform relationships across the LoC and reinventing it as a bridge rather than merely as a boundary-in-the-making.

Notes

[1]   Chaudhri Muhammad Ali, *The Emergence of Pakistan.* New York: Columbia University Press, 1967, p. 319.

[2]   M Ismail Khan, "Skardu Dam: Recipe for Disaster," *The International News,* March 16, 2006.

11

The Growing Alienation in Gilgit-Baltistan: The Future Portents

Alok Bansal

Gilgit-Baltistan in Pakistan occupied Kashmir (POK), termed as 'Northern Areas' by Pakistan has been in turmoil. Legally an Indian territory, the region has become a stage for violent protests by the impoverished population, which believes that their unique ethno-cultural and religious identity is threatened. The discontentment within the populace of 'Northern Areas' has been increasing over the years and besides ethnicity has a strong sectarian undertone. "Rebellion and resentment that have been brewing among people of the Northern Areas, is fast reaching a crescendo against persecution by the Pakistani armed forces, the continuing denial of legal and political rights, and devious attempts at demographic engineering in this strategic region".[1] The people of the region resent the name that Pakistan has given to their region, because it describes them in terms of their geographical position *vis a vis* Pakistani Punjab.

Since 1948, there have been frequent clashes over the ownership of this vital strategic area amongst various ethnic and sectarian groups that are indigenous to the region as well as those that were planted in the region with government connivance from outside. In the last two decades the sectarian divide has been accentuated in the region and there have been numerous reports of mass persecution of people, following different strands of Shiaism. Shias incidentally constitute a majority in Gilgit-Baltistan, unlike Pakistan. In recent past the schools in the region remained closed for a year because different sects could not agree on the contents of the textbooks. There were numerous acts of violence where people invariably targeted the symbols of government authority like police personnel and government officials. These are nothing but growing manifestation of people's discontentment with the Pakistani government. Statements by members of Gilgit Baltistan United Movement where they not only accused Indian government of not doing enough for them but also demanded reservation in Indian educational institutions for the residents of Gilgit-Baltistan,[2] shows the level of their alienation with Pakistan.

Absence of political or legal rights coupled with attempts by successive Pakistani administrators to carry out demographic and sectarian engineering in the region has infuriated the local population. In order to preserve the unique identity of the region Dogra Maharajas had enacted a State Subject Rule, which barred outsiders from seeking permanent residence or naturalisation in the state. However, Bhutto removed it in the 1970s and opened the floodgates of immigration. Interestingly in all other parts of former Kashmir State, the rule is still in force (eg Article 370 in J&K). Outsiders have brought in fundamentalism and madrasa culture. Today Gigit and Baltistan produce more *Ulemas* than a much more populous Punjab. Regular influx of outsiders with government connivance has increased the feeling of insecurity amongst locals.[3]

People perceive the local administration as alien lording over an imperial colony as none of the top officers in police, administration or the government are locals and even at lower level there are a large number of outsiders. Local representation even in Northern Light Infantry, which has been a major source of employment, has been reducing. The region is amongst the most backward in the entire South Asia. Despite being rich in natural resources, the area has failed to reap any benefit and the locals accordingly perceive that their resources are being exploited by the centre without any benefit accruing to them. Bhasha Dam is the newest manifestation of what the locals perceive as the attempt by Islamabad to rob resources from the region to provide them to Punjab and North Western Frontier Province (NWFP). The people feel that their unique cultural and linguistic identity is being marginalised by the large scale influx of outsiders. The feeling is especially strong in Baltistan, where a number of people have started reviving their Tibetan identity. Towards this end they are keen to revive their links with Ladakh and feel that Pakistani establishment is not allowing Kargil- Skardu bus service to prevent their cultural consolidation.[4]

As the alienation with Pakistan rises in this crucial strategic region it will have wider repercussions, which will not be restricted to this region alone. It is therefore essential to analyse the future fall out of growing alienation in this crucial strategic region.

Rise of Separatism

The acts of violence in Gilgit area are indicative of the damage being done to Gigit-Baltistan in the absence of any genuine democratic and constitutional mechanism to solve their problems. "The people feel that they are non-citizens or at best second class citizens." A large number of soldiers from the region lost their lives in the Kargil misadventure of 1999, and has "added a whole new set of grievances."[5] Rampant sectarianism is believed to be the federal government's gift to this region and like in many other parts of Pakistan, the federal government's hand is seen behind sectarian terrorism, which is believed to be a tool being used to divide the people. This deep mistrust of government is the main reason behind attacks on state property and officials, whenever any sectarian incident takes place or any other serious complaint emerges. It is also an indicator of the peoples' lack of ownership of government properties and facilities.

The situation in Gilgit and Baltistan is deteriorating fast. In the face of Pakistani apathy, local grievances have given rise to an ethno-nationalist movement that is rallying the population to reassert the region's unique cultural identity. They would neither like to join an independent Kashmir nor be a part of Pakistan. According to them a separate political entity is essential for preserving their unique ethno-cultural identity.[6] These nationalist groups have been propagating their secessionist views and have been frequently dealt with by the state agencies. There are predominantly two streams of thoughts amongst the nationalist ideologues. The Northern Areas Thinkers' Forum, wants the entire state of Jammu and Kashmir (former princely state) to be divided into two separate entities- "one comprising Azad and held Kashmir minus Ladakh and the second comprising Gilgit-Baltistan-Ladakh".[7] The other group of nationalists aim at establishing an independent 'Balwaristan' consisting of Gilgit, Dardistan and Baltistan. They feel that independence is the only way out of the state repression, poverty, economic exploitation and state sponsored Sunni sectarianism that is being injected in the region with state connivance[8] to threaten its unique ethno-sectarian character. Both the predominant nationalist groups are however, clear that they do not wish to be part of the comprehensive Kashmir package. As the political parties are not permitted to operate in the region, "the nationalist groups like the Balwaristan National Movement have become active to air the grievances of the residents of the area"[9] and the Balwaristan National Movement has gone to the extent of apprising the United Nations (UN) with the local grievances. As the alienation of population grows, the support base for these separatist movements is also growing. They had also petitioned then UN Secretary General Mr Kofi Annan against

Pakistan's sinister move to change the demographic character of the area from a sizeable Shia population, to Pakhtoons brought in from the North West Frontier Province (NWFP).

Spreading Sectarianism

The sectarian violence, which has become endemic in Gilgit-Baltistan, is bound to find its echo in other areas of Pakistan especially in Karachi and NWFP, which are the strongholds of Sunni Deobandi clerics. As it is most of the Deobandi extremists who indulge in violence in Gilgit-Baltistan come from out side and as a result Shia reprisals invariably find their targets in other areas of Pakistan. Similarly, there have been numerous cases where residents of Gilgit-Baltistan were attacked in neighbouring NWFP. As a result in January 2005, when Aga Ziauddin was shot dead, the protests were not confined to the region alone. Islamabad and most other cities saw massive protests. In a tit for tat attack, a Sipah-e-Sahaba cleric was shot dead in Karachi and an attempt was made to kill another Sunni-Deobandi cleric in Islamabad.[10] Even the assassination of General Zia-ul-Haq is believed to be the handiwork of some Shiite Air Force personnel from the region and is an apt example of sectarian violence in Gilgit-Baltistan having its reverberations in Pakistan. Even the journalists who report the events in the region have been threatened and have not been allowed to report faithfully on the happenings there by the sectarian groups.

As Shias are in minority in all other regions of Pakistan, the Shias in Pakistan especially the Ismailis feel concerned about their brethrens in Gilgit-Baltistan, which they perceive as their own region, where they can carry out their own religious experiments. Accordingly Aga Khan Foundation has been quite active in the region and has set up a few educational institutions with their own curriculum. Sunnis especially Deobandis have vociferously opposed the activities of Aga Khan Foundation and have organised protests across the entire length and breadth of Pakistan. *Muttahida Majlis-e-Amal* (MMA) in which both the Sunnis and Shias are represented is engaged in a fierce propaganda campaign against the Aga Khan University Examination Board (AKUEB) these days and believes that AKUEB is an effort "to secularise education in Pakistan".[11] It has accordingly been targeting the Ismaili community. The army disrupted a meeting of the Aga Khan Rural Support Programme in Gilgit on March 20, 2005 on the excuse that the indoor meeting at the local council was violating Section 144. When the indoor nature of the meeting was pointed out by a media man, he was thrashed. The army personnel locked the entire gathering inside the hall for over two hours and misbehaved with those present that included women and children, councillors from different parts of Gilgit and a principal of a degree college.[12] As a result "the Ismaili community today is the most scared local population" and "has been retreating to high altitude localities".[13] Their persecution in Gilgit-Baltistan is bound to have repercussions in other areas even though Ismailis are liberal and not prone to violence. They are, however, fairly prosperous and wield considerable influence in the West.

On account of its unique sectarian composition, the Gilgit-Baltistan has become a sectarian laboratory and the developments in the region have the potential to trigger sectarian violence in entire Pakistan.

Marginalisation of Valley Based Groups in Kashmir

One must appreciate that Gilgit and Baltistan are the constituent of the former princely state of Jammu and Kashmir and will be affected by the final resolution of Kashmir imbroglio. Pakistan for obvious reasons has focussed on Kashmir Valley and has tried to project it as representative of all the parts of the former princely state. According to M Ismail Khan a renowned analyst from the region, of all the parts of the former state, Gilgit-Baltistan is the worst off as unlike other parts, which have been granted some sort of political autonomy and rights by India and Pakistan, this region has been denied "basic political rights and ruled through brute administrative force". According to him the region has "borne the brunt of all four wars over Kashmir. The Kargil conflict left the most devastating scars. Many border villages were destroyed, and every village and town received body bags".[14]

On paper Gilgit and Baltistan are supposed to have a special status, but this special status has only been used to disenfranchise the local population and to usurp their legitimate rights. Despite the special status granted to Gilgit and Baltistan, the region has been placed under martial law, whenever it was enforced in Pakistan, although 'Azad Kashmir' was always kept outside its purview. The region continues to be governed by draconian 'Legal Framework Order' (LFO), which was last promulgated in 1994. The state of Jammu and Kashmir in India not only has its own legislative assembly, it also has its own separate constitution. It also sends representatives to Indian parliament. Similarly, so called 'Azad Kashmir' also has its own constitution and assembly as well as its own nominal 'president' and 'prime minister'. However, these rights have been denied to the residents of Gilgit and Baltistan, who have justifiably been demanding their due share in governance, which is already available to all the other parts of former princely state of Jammu and Kashmir.[15] As their plight has not been projected by Kashmir based outfits propagating independence or separation from India, they do not identify with them and feel that they have no right to represent them. They also feel that they are much worse off than their compatriots.

As the violence intensifies in Gilgit-Baltistan and it comes into the lime light, it will definitely take away the focus from Kashmiri outfits based in Kashmir valley, which over the years have been claiming to represent all parts of the former State of Jammu and Kashmir and all sections of its society. Already, the assertion by the people of the region that All Party Hurriyat Conference (APHC) and other valley based organisations do not represent them[16] is a case in point. Attempts by Jammu and Kashmir Liberation Front (JKLF) and other groups to protest against Bhasha Dam is a belated attempt to gain foothold in the region. However, further alienation in Gilgit-Baltistan will take out the steam from the separatist groups' agenda especially those that espouse the case for a merger with Pakistan. Moreover, sectarian violence in Gilgit-Baltistan will definitely force the Shia minority in the valley to review their commitment to Pakistan.

War against Terror

As the war against terror intensifies in Afghanistan and border areas of Pakistan, a number of senior Al Qaeda leaders are reported to have taken refuse in Chitral and Gilgit- Baltistan. The Sunni fundamentalists in the region and the newly inducted Afghan settlers in Gilgit-Baltistan have strong sympathies bordering on admiration for Al Qaeda. In fact the region is not new to the outfit. In 1988 when then President General Zia-ul-Haq was faced with large scale demonstrations and agitation from Shias in the region against his attempts to introduce Sunni-Deobandi Islam in the region, he had put a Special Service Group (SSG) commanded by then Brigadier Pervez Musharraf to suppress the revolt. It is widely believed that Musharraf responded by transporting "a large number of Wahabi Pakhtoon tribesmen from the NWFP and Afghanistan" who were led by Osama Bin Laden himself, to Gilgit in order "to teach the Shias a lesson". These marauding hordes "massacred hundreds of Shias" in Gilgit and surrounding areas.[17]

As the sectarian turbulence in Gilgit-Baltistan rises the Sunni masses, being numerically inferior are likely to gravitate more and more towards the jihadis led by Al Qaeda. This will increase Al Qaeda and Taliban presence in the region. This in the long term will have an implication on Afghanistan as these elements will use these bases in Gilgit-Baltistan to launch strikes against Afghan targets. This is bound to further strain already tense Pak-Afghan relations. Already Afghan government has been blaming Pakistan of providing shelter to Taliban, and under pressure from the US, the Pakistani government has been forced to crack down on these elements in Waziristan and other parts of Federally Administered Tribal Area (FATA). It, therefore, suits Taliban's sympathizers to shift these elements to Gilgit-Baltistan as it provides them with a chance to show case their success in Waziristan as far as the United States (US) is concerned. On the other hand, their relocation to Gilgit-Baltistan will further marginalise Shias in this strategically region and may further aggravate sectarian tension. Their presence will also increase the fundamentalist influence in the region and wipe off the remnants of the pre-Islamic culture in Gilgit-Baltistan. However, the presence of Al Qaeda and Taliban elements in the region will bring this unknown region on the radar screen of the world community and may even bring sleuths from the US to this mountainous region making it an arena for a new 'Great Game'.

Sino-Pak Relations

Gilgit-Baltistan is the region that links Pakistan to China. Some parts of the region like former State of Hunza have had historical links with China,[18] others like Baltistan have had close links with Tibet. Karakoram Highway is the road link between Pakistan and China. China wants to link up Gwadar to Gilgit and has constructed a dry port at Sust 140 Km North of Gilgit, which was inaugurated by General Musharraf on July 4, 2006.[19] It now intends to expand and realign the Karakoram Highway which will enable it to access the port to facilitate exports from Chinese factories located in north-western China. Gwadar Deep Sea Port project in Balochistan, built with Chinese assistance is located at the mouth of Persian Gulf through which over 40 percent of the world's oil passes, however, the port's financial viability and capacity to become the regional outlet for the growing economies of the landlocked Central Asian Republics lies in reducing the cost and time for movement of goods between Gwadar and Xinjiang.[20] Pakistan aims "to serve as an energy corridor between China and the Gulf". The Karakoram Highway is the most important strategic link between Pakistan and China and has played an important part in cementing the bilateral relationship. Its linkage with the recently built Gwadar Port on Makran Coast will expedite the movement of personnel and cargo between Pakistan and China. The two countries are already planning a rail link between them. "The Chinese have already built the railroad to Tibet. Its extension to Pakistan will lead to a faster movement of cargo and tourists between the two countries".[21]

The turmoil in Gilgit-Baltistan has turned this strategically and economically important highway into a highway of death. The demographic and sectarian struggle in Gilgit-Baltistan has led to the destruction of each other's business entities on the Karakoram Highway that leads up to the Khunjerab Pass and has a direct bearing on the trade from China.[22] Casualties due to bomb explosions, ambushes and sniper firing have become a daily routine and so is the blockade of the Karakoram Highway. At the same time the Chinese have become increasingly concerned about the rising Islamic fundamentalism in Pakistan, which is percolating to Xinjiang province of China dominated by Uighur Muslims. In the past many extremist elements with jihadi bent of mind are reported to have visited the province, which had created furore in Beijing. In order to prevent such radical ideologies from taking roots in society, China was forced to ask Pakistan to rein in these Islamic militants. Some "Chinese students in Pakistani seminaries were repatriated and the Chinese reportedly weeded out hundreds of radical Talibanised Muslim youths in Xinjiang province".[23] As a result the free exchanges between traders in China and Pakistan which was prevalent till the '90s has been curtailed. Thereafter, the visa regime for ordinary Pakistani border traders was tightened and the number of Pakistani traders travelling to Xinjiang has gone down considerably.

Though the visa regime had remained relatively liberal for the residents of Gilgit and Baltistan, the recent violence has changed all that. The Chinese have become apprehensive of the rising fundamentalism in the region and are extremely cautious in allowing people from the region to enter Chinese territory. The resultant strong handed treatment by the Chinese officials at the border check posts has caused lot of consternation amongst the Pakistani officials and general public, which had travelled by the recently introduced bus service to Kashgar. As a result there are now reports that the bus service will be closed down within a month of its starting with much fanfare.[24] Chinese are extremely wary of Islamic fundamentalism seeping into Xinjiang from this region and any turmoil in the region will have a bearing on Sino-Pak relations. The area around Karakoram Highway from Gilgit to China border is dominated by the Shia militants whereas, the area South West of Gilgit up to Manshera is under the influence of Sunni extremists. Some of them have sympathies for Uighur nationalists in Xinjiang and may be inclined to attack Chinese vehicles passing through the Highway. Any attack on the Chinese vehicles or assassination of Chinese personnel on or around the Highway may cause Pakistan a huge embarrassment and generate adverse publicity for Pakistan.[25] As the Chinese trade through Karakoram Highway increases it will become more sensitive to the acts of violence and disruption of traffic on this crucial highway, where they have invested lot of resources. As it is a number of inhabitants of region especially in Hunza valley are unhappy with Sino-Pak accord of 1963, which gave away a portion of the territory under the control of erstwhile State of Hunza to China, without even taking the local population into confidence. They were even suspicious of Chinese presence in the region during construction of Karakoram Highway.[26] Growing Talibanisation and sectarian rift in a region that links China to Pakistan therefore has the potential to derail Sino-Pak relations.

Indo-Pak Relations

In case the violence and alienation in Gilgit and Baltistan increase, it will have its bearing on India Pakistan relations. Already a number of Pakistani government spokespersons and media reports have talked of external involvement in the region. In a carefully considered move, the Indian government criticised Pakistan's unwillingness to ever hold elections in Gilgit and Baltistan. It also objected to the construction of Bhasha Dam in a disputed territory. The government also criticised Pakistan's harassment of leaders from Gilgit and Baltistan who had recently visited India. In June 2006, the government again slammed Islamabad's disqualification of candidates, who refused to take an oath of support to Kashmir's accession to Pakistan, in the elections to the so called 'Azad Kashmir' assembly in July 2006.

For a long time after Shimla Agreement of 1972, India had turned a blind eye to the developments in Pakistan occupied Kashmir. It had ignored the decision in Islamabad to separate Gilgit and Baltistan from the POK and keep it in a constitutional limbo. It also refused to react to the developments within POK and expected Pakistan to do the same on Jammu and Kashmir. While New Delhi resented Pakistan's intervention in Jammu and Kashmir, it dithered about paying back in the same coin. The new Indian focus on Gilgit and Baltistan and 'Azad Kashmir' would create a more balanced negotiating framework with Pakistan. This should also help India raise the national awareness on the many ignored dimensions of Kashmir and educate the international community on the complexity of the dispute. Above all, it sends out a long-delayed message to the people of Gilgit, Baltistan and the 'Azad Kashmir' that India will not be a mute spectator to the injustices being perpetrated on them by Islamabad.[27]

Pakistan realises that it is on a weak wicket as far as the region is concerned. Accordingly it has been reluctant to start Kargil-Skardu bus service, even though it will unite the divided families and provide enormous economic opportunities to the people of the region. It will provide a more reliable road link to a region that remains cut off from rest of the world for most of the year. However, the starting of bus service between Kargil and Skardu may expose the population of the region to the freedom and democratic rights being enjoyed by their ethnic kin across the Line of Control in Ladakh and Kargil. To quote M Ismail Khan from popular Pakistani daily *The News:* "the people in Ladakh are perhaps, a little more involved, empowered and relaxed. This may well be a reason why Pakistan is not so enthusiastic about opening to Ladakh".[28] For these reasons the revival of old routes with Ladakh might not suit General Musharraf, who came close to accepting Gilgit and Baltistan as part of 'Azad Kashmir' in his controversial seven point formula for talks on Kashmir.[29]

Conclusion

The decision to build Bhasha Dam on River Indus, which will lead to inundation of vast areas in Diamer district of Gilgit-Baltistan, has the potential to further alienate population in this restive region. After almost six decades of being under Pakistani occupation, the population of the region continues to be denied its rightful constitutional rights. The region is neither a province, nor does it have the status the other part of POK so called 'Azad Kashmir' enjoys with its own legislative assembly. The growing alienation of population has led to the rise of separatist movements in Gilgit-Baltistan. Frustration arising from unemployment and discrimination is acting as catalyst for people to come out on the streets. As the region has been kept outside the jurisdiction of courts, the people receive no redress. An indifferent bureaucracy, and political leadership, and an oppressive Army, have all put Gilgit and Baltistan on a turbulent course, which may not be possible to change. Due to a very low literacy level, extreme poverty and no organised political activity, the Ulema has acquired a strong hold over the people. This has led to sectarian polarisation and frequent eruption of violence across sectarian divide. However, this sectarian violence often spills over to various parts of Pakistan.

Due to the strategic location of the region the alienation in the region affects all the countries surrounding it and has the potential to affect Pakistan's relations both with China and Afghanistan. The turbulence in the region may also attract Al Qaeda and other jihadis besides remnants of Taliban and may force Pakistani Army and the US to shift their focus from Waziristan and FATA to Gilgit-Baltistan. Not only does the growing alienation in the region affects the ultimate resolution of Jammu and Kashmir, it has the potential to marginalise the valley based groups who have traditionally claimed to represent all parts and sections of Jammu and Kashmir. The growing alienation in the region has not only invited the charges of external interference from Pakistan, it has also provided India a valuable leverage against Pakistan and, therefore, has the capability to affect Indo-Pak relations. Thus to conclude, as the alienation in the region increases it will have far reaching effects on the entire region and has the potential to change the social, political and economic geography of the region.

Notes.

1   "Northern Areas: A tale of neglect, Denial?" from *New Indian Express* Website http://www.newindpress.com/NewsItems. asp?ID=IEP20060529092431&Page=P&Title=Nation& Topic=0 (Accessed on May 30, 2006).

2   Ibid.

3   Alok Bansal, "Gilgit-Baltistan : The forgotten Part of J&K", *SAPRA India Bulletin*, July 2006, p 10.

4   Ibid.

5   Zaigham Khan, "Gilgit on Fire", *The International News,* Internet Edition, January 15, 2005.

6   Moonis Ahmar, "Kashmir's Identity Crisis", *The News,* Rawalpindi, March 2, 2004.

7   M Ilyas Khan. "Disagree and Be Damned", *The Herald*, Karachi, December 2000, p 43.

8   Stephen Philip Cohen. *The Idea of Pakistan* , Oxford University Press, New Delhi, 2005, pp 222-223.

9   Amjad Bashir Siddiqi, "Conflict in Gilgit", *The International News*, Internet Edition, November 14, 2005.

10 Wison John, "Unrest in Gilgit : New Challenge for Musharraf", *ORF Strategic Trends*, Volume III, Issue 19, dated May 16, 2005 from ORF Website http://www.observerindia.com/strategic/st050516.htm (Accessed on June 30, 2006).

11 Shahzad Shah, "AKU exam board to start work despite opposition", *The Herald*, April 2005, p 51.

12 Farman Ali, "Army personnel beat up journalist in Skardu", *The Herald*, April 2005, p 44.

13 Khaled Ahmed, "The Sectarian State in Gilgit", *The Friday Times*, July 15-21, 2005, p 8.

14 M Ismail Khan, "Demystifying Kashmir", *The International News,* Internet Edition January 23, 2006.

15 M Ismail Khan, "Northern Areas and the Charter", *The International News*, Internet Edition, May 28, 2006.

16 SP Sharma, " Hurriyat does not represent entire J&K: PoK website", *The Tribune*, Chandigarh, August 27, 2006.

17 B Raman, "Biography of General Pervez Musharraf: His Past and Present" from Website http://www.angelfire.com/al4/terror/musharraf.htm (Accessed on June 26, 2006).

18 FM Hassnain, *Gilgit : The Northern Gate of India*, New Delhi: Sterling Publishers Pvt Ltd, 1978, pp 41-42. . •

19 Safdar Khan, "Karakoram Highway's Gwadar link likely", *Dawn*, Karachi, July 5, 2006.

20 M Ismail Khan, "Beijing to Kashgar, Gilgit to Gwadar", *The International News*, Internet Edition, March 1, 2006.

21 "Gwadar-KKH link", Editorial, *Dawn*, July 6, 2006.

22 Khaled Ahmed, no 13.

23 M Ismail Khan, no 20.

24 "Suspension of Sino-Pak bus service feared amid lack of facilities", http://www.onlinenews.com.pk/details.php?id =99110 (Accessed on June 27, 2006).

25 Alok Bansal, "Karakoram Impasse", *The Pioneer*, New Delhi, May 30, 2005, p 8.

26 Samuel Baid, "Northern Areas" in Jasjit Singh (ed), *Pakistan Occupied Kashmir: Under The Jackboot*, New Delhi, Siddhi Books, 1995, p 134.

27 "India's new assertiveness on POK is thanks to its peace offensive with Pakistan", *The Indian Express*, June 15, 2006.

28 M Ismail Khan, "Why not Kargil", *The International News*, Internet Edition, September 6, 2005.

29 Vinod Sharma, "Pakistan's Guantanamo", *The Hindustan Times*, New Delhi, December 21, 2004, p. 10.

Index